CONVERSATIONS WITH
SATHYA SAI BABA

Dr. John Hislop

Birth Day Publishing Company
San Diego, California, U.S.A.

This book may be obtained at your local bookstore or you may order it directly from Birth Day Publishing Company, at a cost of $6.30 plus $1.00 for postage and handling. Send check or money order to Birth Day Publishing Company, P. O. Box 7722, San Diego, California 92107.

Library of Congress Catalog Number 79-51262

ISBN 0-9600958-5-3

Published by Birth Day Publishing Company
P.O. Box 7722, San Diego, California 92107, USA

DEDICATION

This work is submitted at the Lotus Feet of Sri Sathya Sai, who is as a Lighthouse to me, buffeted as I am by gails of ignorance and tossed here and there amidst the stormy shoals of my life. The signal from Light is: Abandon the stormy shallows for the Deep, for therein is to be found calm and bliss everlasting, and liberation from the snarl of birth and death. Indeed, Sri Sathya Sai declares that Love is the Deep, and that Love itself is God.

"Your Reality is the Atma (God viewed as the particular), a wave of the Paramatma (God viewed as the Universal). The one object of this human existence is to visualize that Reality, that Atma, that relationship between the Wave and the Sea. All other activities are trivial; you share them with birds and beasts; but, this is the unique privilege of Man. He has clambered through all the levels of animality, all the steps in the ladder of evolution in order to inherit this high destiny. If his years between birth and death are frittered away in seeking food, shelter, comfort and pleasure as animals do, man is condemning himself to a further life sentence.

"For, the individual and the Universal are one; the wave is the sea. Merging fulfills. When merged, the ego is dissolved; all symbols and signs of the particular, like name, form, caste, color, creed, nationality, church, sect and the rights and duties consequent thereon, will fade. For such individuals, who have liberated themselves from the narrowness of individuality, the only task is the uplifting of humanity, the welfare of the world, and the showering of love. Even if they are quiet, the state of Bliss in which they are will shower bliss on the world. Love is in all; Love is of all; Love is all.

"When people forget the One and run after the many, Dharma declines; for, there can be no love, no sacrifice, no detachment in human affairs then. So, the Lord takes human form and comes to restore man's sense of values. You may ask, why should the Lord Himself incarnate? Why can He not set about the task of restoring Dharma through the pantheon of beings He has at His command? This very question was posed before the courtiers by Akbar himself, for he laughed at the Hindu idea of the Formless adopting Form and descending into the world as an Avatar to save Dharma. Tansen asked for a week's time to furnish the answer, and got the time granted by His Imperial Majesty. A few days later, when he was in the pleasure boat of the Emperor sailing across the lake with the Emperor's family, Tansen cleverly threw overboard a doll made to look like the Emperor's little son, crying at the same time, 'Oh, the Prince has fallen into the water!' Hearing this, the Emperor jumped into the lake to rescue his son!

"Tansen then disclosed that it was only a doll and that the son was safe. He allayed the anger of Akbar by explaining that he had perforce to enact this drama in order to demonstrate the truth of the Hindu belief that God takes human form, Himself, to save Dharma, without commissioning some other entity to carry out that task. Dharma is as the son, God loves it so dearly. Akbar could have ordered one among the many personnel he had on board to jump in and rescue his son; but his affection was so great and the urgency so acute that the Emperor himself plunged into the lake to pull out the 'son.' The decline in Dharma is so acute a tragedy, the intensity of affection that the Lord has for good men is so great, that He Himself comes. The Lord is Love Itself. He comes in human form so that you can talk to Him, move with Him, serve Him, adore Him, and achieve Him, so that you can recognize your kinship with Him.

"I declare that I am in every one, in every being. So do not hate anyone or cavil at anyone. Spread Love always, everywhere. That is the way of revering me. Do not seek to measure me or evaluate me. I am beyond your understanding. Pray or worship for your own satisfaction and contentment. But, to say that I will respond only if I am called, or that I will save only if I am thought of is wrong. Have you not heard the declaration, 'Sarvathah panni paadam'? 'You can hear my footsteps, for I walk with you, behind you, beside you.' When you cry out in agony, 'Don't you hear my heart's plaint? Have you become so stony-hearted?' My ear will be there to listen. Ask that I should protect you like the apple of My eye, and My eye will be there to watch over you and guard you. I answer to whatever Name you use; I respond to whatever request you make with a pure heart and a sanctified motive."

Sathya Sai Baba

"You must have heard of people seeking moksha (liberation) and getting moksha, and many may be under the impression that it is some rare honor that only a few secure, or that it is some area like paradise or a colony of the elect, or a height that some heroic souls alone can climb up to. No; moksha is something that all must achieve, whether they are heroic or not; even those who deny it have to end by realizing it. For, everyone is even now seeking it when he seeks joy and peace; and who does not seek joy and peace? Moksha is when you have lasting joy and lasting peace. Tired with temporary joys and transient peace, man will at last endeavor to know the secret of permanent joy and peace—that is to say, moksha. If only men knew the path to permanent joy and peace, they would not wander distracted among the bye-lanes of sensual pleasure. This essential teaching is absent in modern curricula; men and women live many years without knowing the secret of joyful, peaceful living. The educated are today more discontented than the uneducated, whereas they ought really to be calmer and less subject to the agitations of the mind.

"You must tackle this problem straight from where it starts. Ignorance can be cured only by knowledge; darkness can be destroyed only by light—no amount of argument or threat or persuasion can compel darkness to move away. A flash of light, that is enough; darkness is gone. Prepare for that flash of illumination; the light is there already in you. But, since it is heavily overladen by repressing factors, it cannot reveal itself. 'The liberation from night' which happens when the Light is revealed, is called Moksha. Everyone has to achieve it, whether he is striving for it now or not. It is the inevitable end to the struggle, the goal towards which all are proceeding.

"Well, how do you prepare yourself for that stage? I must tell you that the answer is in that very word, moksha, itself. It is self explanatory. 'Mo' indicates 'Moha' (delusion; being deluded by the scintillating, the gaudy, the transitory, the temporary trash); and 'Ksha' means 'Kshaya' (decline; disappearance; destruction). It requires you to keep the flights of your mind away from these deluding attractions and on the straight path towards liberation."

Sathya Sai Baba

FOREWORD

The questions and answers included here date from January, 1968, through February, 1978. The first two interviews were taped and are reproduced in full. Thereafter, notes were made from memory immediately after each conversation.

The questions asked make no pretence of being profound. The answers, however, come directly from Truth and may illumine the understanding of the greatest scholar or the most practiced yogi.

Devotees are aware how infrequent and difficult to secure are conversations with Bhagawan; for this reason, a decision was made to publish the notebook.

Except for the two taped interviews, questions and answers are not in chronological order. Definitions of all Sanskrit and Telugu words are provided in the Glossary at the end of the book.

J. S. Hislop.

I

Taped Interview, January, 1968

Hislop: We do not perceive life with absolute clarity, and yet we are acting all the time, and unclear action makes for a confused life. We are unhappy about that confusion, and in an effort to remove it we accumulate ideas of truth, God, reality. But those imaginings do not remove the confusion. Life is still confused. So the question, what is the big factor that prevents us from seeing the truth of life clearly?

Sai: You say that truth, God, reality are imagination. Why do you think they are imagination? They are not. Time, work, reason and experience: these four in harmony together, that is truth. When the four are found not to be in harmony, then you feel it is untruth. An example: Yesterday you came to Bangalore and from there to Puttaparthi by car. Travel is work. It took you four hours to come from Bangalore. That is time. You came to see Swami. That is the reason. Having seen Him, you got happiness. That is the result.

On the other hand, last night you dreamed that you were in

America and were shopping. In this, the four factors were not involved. There was no work, there was no time expended, and where is the result? This is untruth. That experience was imagination, only mind work. This is the difference between truth and imagination.

H: But truth, that is in terms of work, time, reason and result—you look around the world and you see those things in operation, and the world is in a mess. So, there must be more to it than that?

Sai: When you don't have absolute faith in the result, then doubt arises. An example: Now it is daylight and the objects in the room are seen very clearly, and there is no doubt in regards to them. At night when it is fully dark and you have to grope around and do not see any of the objects, there is no doubt about that situation. But at dusk, when it is half light and half dark, doubt can arise and you may see a rope and imagine it to be a snake and have fear.

Light is not full and vision is not clear. Full light is wisdom, and full dark is ignorance. Doubt arises when there is half dark and half light. The half light is wisdom, and the half dark is ignorance. Ignorance and wisdom: when there is half and half, there is doubt. Now you are in the middle stage where you have this little bit of wisdom and also some ignorance. Now you are in this middle stage where ignorance and wisdom are mixed. You are not fully experienced. When you have proper experience, the doubt will vanish. Because you are not experienced, you are having this doubt.

A small example: While suffering from malaria, you have eaten a sweet but feel it has a bitter taste. It was not that the sweet was bitter, but in your experience it was bitter. It is not the fault of the sweet. Ignorance is also a disease like malaria. And the cure for this disease of ignorance is sadhana. Man has doubt only while he does not know the truth. Once you experience the truth, doubt will vanish. Truth is one, and for all time truth is truth. Whatever changes, know that as untruth.

Once you were small and you grew bigger. That is also

untruth. Where is the body of the ten-year-old? All has merged into the present body. First, untruth; then, when we have the experience, we know the truth. Dark and light are not different; they are one only. A small example: Last night you ate fruit. In the morning it becomes stool and you pass it out. It was fruit yesterday, but the bad and the good are the same, only one. In one form, it was fruit, in the other form it was stool.

It is the same with light and dark. When the light comes, the darkness goes. But really, the darkness does not go anyplace and the light does not go anyplace. When one comes, the other is unknown; it does not go anywhere.

H: This mixture of light and darkness, of ignorance and wisdom which creates unhappiness, which creates trouble— Swami says that the mixture fades away with the right experience. The question is, what is the basic factor that prevents us from having that right experience?

Sai: We don't have the intensity that is required. Even to study books, how much is needed to come to the stage when we can read difficult books. How many years, how many hours of toil we put into it. If you have the same intensity in spiritual practice, you will surely know the truth. But we are not as intense as we should be on the spiritual path. We do not apply concentration and one-pointedness. Full concentration is needed, even in the world, in walking, talking, reading. Without concentration you cannot do anything. Even in little things of the world we use concentration.

But when we try to think of God, then we get restless, and the mind is unstable. Why do we do the things of the world with full concentration? Why? Because we are fully interested in it. And with God we have these doubts. In whatever work you love deeply, you have full concentration. In whatever you don't love deeply, then concentration is not full.

A small example: You are driving a car. And at the same time you are talking to your passengers. The road becomes narrow and dangerous. You say, 'Please let us not talk now, I must give full concentration to the driving.' Why do you say

3

this? It is because you deeply love your life and you must concentrate deeply so as to avoid an accident. Because you have this love for body, you concentrate on its safety. When you have deep love for God, then concentration on Him will come automatically.

H: But that is the point, there is the whole point.

Sai: In all these experiences, we must hold to the truth, to life. You love life. Because of life we have all these experiences. So we cling to that sort of pillar which is life; for we know that without life we don't have experiences. Life gives so many things externally, but life does not change. Life is the same—that life is truth and that is God. The unchangeable is truth.

H: Since we are that truth, we would like to have love in our hearts and flow naturally with life and not according to our arbitrary wishes. Yet, we don't. Swami says we do not, because we lack the intensity. So we say to ourselves, 'Well, I must get that intensity.' So we strive towards that goal, and striving towards that goal makes the thing stronger and that prevents the desired intensity.

Translator: I don't follow that.

H: We are selfish and greedy naturally. If we substitute a spiritual goal for a physical goal, then we are still engaged in the same greed. One has just changed the physical greed to spiritual greed. A further point: If one does not love, as indeed one does not, then one says, 'I must get love.' Then love is over there and oneself is here.

Sai: Who are you? Who are you?

H: I am the accumulation of all my past, all my ideas.

Sai: Who is that 'my'? Who is that 'my'? Who is that 'my' who is claiming? Between the love and yourself there is this claim. What is love and who are you?

H: I am that which I am, the accumulation of all these . . .

H's wife: The accumulation is the idea that you have, but according to Swami, you and the love are the same thing. You are the one who makes the separation.

4

H: Yes, I am the one who puts the separation between us. I am the ego.

Sai: Ego is untruth.

H: Ego is untruth, then I . . .

Sai: But you are not ego. You are truth. Ego is not truth. Any amount of arguments and discussions like this is just words. You will not get this without spiritual practice, without sadhana. An example: Someone asks us what sugar is. We say it is brownish and sort of sandy, because we know sugar. But the sweetness has no form. Like that you can describe sugar, but you cannot picture the taste, because the taste has no form.

Even pertaining to the world, there are so many things we do not know, and we don't imagine or worry about it. If we only feel intensely for God instead of so much discussion and reading books. We must get into the field and try it out. Even if someone writes a book, it is *his* spiritual experience. You love your wife and she loves you. But if she is hungry, you cannot eat for her. And if you are hungry, she cannot eat for you despite the fact that you love each other dearly. Spiritual hunger is like that. Each man must seek and appease that hunger according to his faith.

Even though Swami tries to explain, you do not grasp it. It is only through experience you must come to it. When you start to learn to drive, you must have an open space for practice; but once you learn, then even on a narrow road you can go with confidence. It is just like in a school. Gradually you go and you understand. If big words are used, the child does not understand them when he is still learning the A B C's.

In the beginning, we do not understand things of the world and do not even understand ourselves, so how can you understand that which is beyond you? So, first you try to understand yourself by doing spiritual practice, by doing sadhana. First 'I,' next 'You.' 'I' plus 'You' equals 'We.' Then 'We' plus 'He.' Then only 'He.'

H: No. I don't understand that.

Sai: First 'I,' then 'You.' First 'I'; that is life. Next 'You';

that is the world. 'I' plus 'You' is 'We.' 'We' plus 'He' is God. Then only 'He.' There is love, the person who loves, and the person you love. And when all get together, it is bliss. You see, there are three blades in the fan. The three gunas are represented by the three blades. Only when the blades circulate together in harmony do you get the air. When they move in the same direction they bring the cool air. Within us, the three gunas are going all in different directions. When you turn them in the same direction, all going around together, then you will get the one-pointedness and you will be enabled to know.

A Visitor: Could it be like this? It is the experience of a number of people, including myself, that one does sadhana gradually. But then suddenly comes such an experience, that ordinarily would have taken an immense time. Does it come suddenly because of Your grace?

Sai: Another example: In a house, each one does a particular job and divides the work. In the evening when the family has finished the work, nobody says, 'Father, I did such and such work and you must pay me.' It is one house, so you don't ask for payment, you just do the work. But when people from outside come to do work, you fix the rate and pay accordingly. When you pay them, that shows they are outsiders. But when they are your own, you don't have to pay them. They work with interest and no pay is expected.

Similarly with God. When you think God is the nearest and dearest to you, like one family, you don't ask for pay. The one who surrenders like that, he is My own, he does not have to look for payment. But the one who says, 'I have done so much sadhana,' and barters with God and says, 'I have done so much sadhana and you should give me such and such a reward,' then that is the difference; he is an outsider.

The child who is small does not ask the mother, 'I want milk, I want to be changed,' and so on, but the mother looks after every need of the child without its asking. When you have surrendered yourself completely to God and become God's child, you don't have to tell God what you want. He will give

6

even more than you have asked for. But it is only by love that He is your dearest. Do sadhana and there is a closeness to God; then you don't have to tell Him that you want this or that. Because you are like a little child, He will come and give you more than even what you ask for.

Ego is what prevents us from getting close to God. It is that ego: 'I' have to do this, 'I' have to get all this. You must see that 'I' am only the instrument of the Lord. Like the fan is an instrument, you are an instrument of the Lord. Now, is the fan making the fan rotate, or is the current making the fan rotate?

H: The curent is making the fan rotate.

Sai: The current is God, so you are only the instrument. Even the fact that we think that our eyes see things and our ears hear things: that is not correct. My eyes are here, but the mind is in Bangalore, thinking of this or that. My eyes see, but my mind is somewhere else. Mind is important. The body is like a flashlight; the eye is the bulb; mind is the battery cell; intelligence is the switch. Only when the four work together do you get the light.

H: Surrender to God is everything, of course, but . . .

Sai: The word, 'surrender,' in English, is not quite correct, it is not the right word. It does not quite explain. When you say, 'surrender,' you are separate and God is separate. That is the meaning you get. But God is not separate.

A Visitor: The word 'surrender' is not the correct word, so self-realization . . .

Sai: Self-realization—that is why they call it so. You realize your own Self. You are you, not your wife. You are You.

A Second Visitor: Where is our responsibility? We are supposed to share, to help others.

A Third Visitor: Help oneself first.

Sai: 'Self' is the base or foundation. 'Help' is the wall. God is the roof or top of the building. Light is the owner.

A Visitor: But she was asking, 'What is the limit?' Where is the limit of one's responsibility? How far should she go?

Sai: First you should look after yourself and not be a burden. That is the first thing. If you are not able to help so many people, it doesn't matter. But if you don't do anything that is harmful, that is real help. If you can't help a person, never mind. But don't harm anybody. To harm is bad. But the very feeling that you have that you can't help, itself is good. You must have physical strength, mental strength, and spiritual strength; and only when you have the three, then can you really do service. Food, head, and God. Food is for the body; and you want a good body so the brain can function properly, so you can think. And why do you want this head and intellect? To realize that which is beyond this, and that is God.

Visitor: But it hurts me to see people in need, beggars and innocent little children who are ill . . .

A second Visitor: Is it not egoistic to have everything for yourself?

Translator: But Swami did not mean that. What Swami said is that when you do not have the physical, mental and spiritual strength, how can you really help another person?

Sai: Sometimes when we are not balanced and have not got the proper truth, we will mislead so many other people.

A Visitor: It is that you cannot give what you do not have.

A Second Visitor: Nothing before straightening yourself.

H: Is it possible for Swami to give the lady self-realization?

A Third Visitor: Swami says it is possible. Since He gives the truth, can He not also give self-realization to the heart?

Sai: When there is that feeling, that depth of feeling, Swami can give it. Oh, yes. She has such a depth of feeling for the body. If she has the same intensity for God-realization, Swami can give it. Just now.

H: So that is what Swami means by, 'Before you can help people.'

Sai: The more intensity, the greater the result. If you are digging a well, the deeper you dig, the higher will be the wall formed by the mud you bring out. The depth is in the form of the height.

8

H: Swami says that He cannot give to a dry heart. Why is the heart dry?

Sai: Even that, God gives for our own good. When you don't have hunger, why should He give you food? When you have hunger and receive food, it is useful, but if you don't have hunger and He gives food, you will have indigestion. Sometimes, even if you have hunger, God does not give food to you. Just to keep you in check and in control.

Suppose you are in the hospital. They can't give you everything you might ask for. There is a proper time and the proper way for your own sake. Even a spiritual experience—sometimes God withholds it, because God does everything for man's good. He never does anything to harm man or give him sorrow. But that faith you must have. First you must grapple with the fact that duty is God, and start doing your duty.

H: Is it that the heart is dry because one is not doing his duty?

Sai: No man's heart is really dry. At least men have "sense" love—you have worldly love for children, family and others. It is the same love, but given to some only. You only have to take it all and give it to God.

A Visitor: If his heart were completely dry, he would not want to come to Prasanthi Nilayam.

Sai: Even in coming to Prasanthi Nilayam, you could be loving your wife and family. Live in love. Love itself is God. He is nothing else but love. There are different forms of love, love for family and love for money; but love for God is devotion. There is a glass of water. An English man will call it water, an Andhra man will call it by another name, and in Tamil still another name is given. But the water is the same. We just call it by different names.

The names of love for wife, children, objects differ, and love for God is called devotion, but the love is one. The most important thing you have to develop is love. If you develop love, you don't have to develop anything else.

9

H: But love is not something made by man. Love is not something created by man; how can I develop love?

Sai: You have love for the tape recorder. How is it that you have that love? When the tape recorder was in the shop, did you love it? But because you have got it now, it is yours, 'my' tape recorder. You did not love it in the shop; you love it now because you feel it is 'mine.' So, when you think God is 'mine,' you love Him.

A Visitor: I make an effort to strengthen love, but I know it does not happen.

Sai: It is a question of practice. Intellectually you understand. Say you have a temperature, a 105-degree fever. If you keep on chanting 100 times, 'I want a penicillin injection,' it won't cure you. You have to have the injection. You don't have to chant that you want penicillin; you just have to have one poke and you are all right. Instead of thinking of ten different things to do, if you do one thing correctly, that is enough. When you are thirsty, you don't want all the water from the well. One glass will suffice. You don't have to take all and try to practice everything. Take one. Here is a match box with some 60 matches, if you want to light a fire you need to strike one match, not the entire box of matches.

H: Swami, in the hospital, each patient has a principal disease; is the doctor able to know that principal disease?

Sai: If he is a good doctor, yes. If he just has a degree, no. In present-day India in the political field, people have studied very little; but because of politics they get a doctor degree.

H: Then let the Supreme Doctor tell me what my chief disease is—not physical.

Sai: You do have this desire to go towards God. But you are just at the point where you want to know, 'How to go to it.' This, Swami cannot say before the others. He will say to you separately. Such problems are separate. Like the doctor, each patient he examines separately, not while everyone is in the room.

A Visitor: Swami, do I continue teaching the same meditation? There are not always the same people there.

Sai: You must have the same group. Then if new people come, you must give them a separate time and not mix them with the others.

Visitor: Yesterday there were a number of new people.

Sai: There is not much difference within the group. Even the people who come to you do not know much. If the child wants to learn the A B C's, he must continue to say A, B, C, D, and so on.

A Visitor: When should I leave?

Sai: Whatever your decision is. If you want to leave on the 19th morning, Swami will see you tomorrow. But if you have other plans, it will be adjusted accordingly. Swami is not limited by space. Wherever you are, here or in Bombay or wherever, He is with you. You have to be happy. That is what Swami wants. So it should depend on your decision.

Visitor: But I am a person for whom decisions are a great difficulty.

Sai: The human problem is this: of deciding good and bad all the time. You can leave the 19th morning.

A Second Visitor: Swami, I have been away from business and I want to talk with Swami, but if I stay another month, then there will be only one final talk with Swami. I want to talk with Swami now, and then stay a month.

Sai: Tomorrow is Thursday. Swami will see each of you individually, then you can make your plans, when you want to leave or whether you want to stay. With you, it is like this: You have a few doubts; now you want to clear those doubts immediately so as to leave room for new doubts (much merriment from the interview group). That is your plan.

Sai (to a Visitor): You have some plan for poor people. What are the details?

Visitor: The old Mandir. We should make a number of new homes for the poor people. Then those who are now staying in the old Mandir can move to the new houses and the old temple

11

can be made like new. It is Swami's first Mandir and it should be saved for history. If people continue to live there, it will tumble down in no time at all. To use it just for living looks like a lack of respect from the people who are in Puttaparthi.

Sai: That can be discussed further at a later time. Now, Swami is troubled that all of you have come from so far and have spent so much—your love is so touching. There is no price for that love even if measured in crores and crores. Swami wants your happiness. Swami will teach as quickly as possible.

Visitor: But now is the time because there is the world conference in May and Swami's devotees will come here. It does not matter whose plan it is to save the old Mandir; it should be as though it is everyone's idea and all should work together to accomplish it.

Sai: You draw up a plan and show it to Swami—how to do it.

Visitor: And one other thing: I must ask Swami because people say Swami must be asked. I want a little plot of land. On the opposite hill if I have a little place and then put a big shed— I have the plan—so that there is a big place where they can come and gather and do yoga or whatever it is. But then when I am so close—that is, closer than from here to the old Mandir, but not just outside the gate so that people will be saying this or that about me—then I am outside, and then—you know . . .

A visitor interrupts: . . . so that no control . . .

A Second Visitor: No control . . .

Sai: A faithless garden. (Much merriment from the interview group.)

Visitor: Well, you know, nobody can come and say, 'No cooking,' and so on.

Sai: It might be all right to start, but then you will have many more problems than you wish for: all the dogs from the villages and other problems.

Visitor: The thing is what I have said at home, that I would like to have a little house outside the compound.

Sai: With all the dogs together, you are going to have a great problem. Ten puppies each.

Visitor: But, anyway, you . . .

Sai: We will discuss it. You may start enthusiastically, but then the problems that will be coming in the future will not be good.

(Swami now moves His hand, and a large mass of sugar-candy appears in His hand and is distributed. The group exclaims how sweet and delightful it tastes.)

Sai: Complete sugar.

Visitor: Not only sugar. It is flavoured.

Sai: Every day should be sweet like this, that Swami would again make sugar.

Visitor: Someone told me that I should not let anybody touch these earrings that you gave me, because they are sacred. But I don't like to tell people not to touch.

Sai: Nothing like that, about touching. Was everyone angry because Swami did not come this morning?

Visitor: No, no, Baba. We were singing bhajans and talking about the gopis.

Sai: Gopi means sense control, one who has controlled the senses. It is not a lady's name.

End of Interview

II

A second taped interview was conducted the next day. Both interviews were in the third week of January, 1968.

H: What does surrender to the Lord mean in such common things as shaving, going to the market, walking and so on?

Sai: Surrendering to the Lord is surrendering all thoughts and actions, not wishing for the fruits of the action, not doing action to gain its fruit but doing the action because it is one's

13

duty. The act is dedicated to the Lord and the results, therefore, are borne by the Lord. Actions done thus—fruits abandoned at the time of the action—such action is free of karma. Since the ego, in this way, is not fed and cultivated, it disappears before long. For example, if one shaves, which is classed as an uninspired mundane task, the attitude is that one is preparing the body for the sake of the Lord in the heart, and one is making the best of his appearance to honor the Lord, and not for one's personal vanity or reward. Also, in walking, offer the action to the Lord to maintain a body fit for the Lord to live in; and that is the attitude for every single act of the day.

Sweeping the house is dedicated to the Lord so that He may have a fit dwelling. And cooking also is dedicated to Him so that the body may be strong and vigorous for the benefit of the Lord. It is folly to seek the fruit of action. When one dies, the only items taken with one are one's good and bad deeds. None of the power, the money, the position, the prestige, the vigorous beauty of the body, the culture of the personality— these things are all gone, and therefore what folly to work for them. Man is life with desire; life without desire is God. Mind is desire; when mind disappears, desire disappears.

H: Swami, a taxi will arrive here for us on the afternoon of the 26th for our departure.

Sai: No, no, that is wrong. When you come from so far to see Sai and then take a taxi for Bangalore, Sai is shamed. It should be left for Sai to take care. You should not do it yourselves.

H: I will cancel the taxi at once.

Sai: In the last day or so there have been riots in Bangalore by students protesting the campaign by northern politicians to make Hindi the national language instead of English. There were bomb-throwings and other violence. It might be better for you and your wife to leave here on the 25th instead of the 26th because on the 26th a high northern official will be arriving, and probably there will be more rioting.

H: What is meant when Swami says to a departing devotee

14

that, 'Swami will be with you wherever you are; Swami is in your heart'?

Sai: The situation can be compared to a man and a stick floating in the ocean. Both have the same motion, up and down with the waves; but the stick does not know what is happening, whereas the man is conscious of the movement. The movement of the stick could be compared to a person in America in whose heart God resides but who has never been here to visit Swami. The conscious movement of a man swimming in the ocean could be compared to an American who has visited here and then returned home. Now there would be conscious spiritual experience and that would be the case whether we consciously invited that experience or not.

There are three stages to knowing God. One is intellect, which is just imagination; one is drawing near; and third is union with God. Another example: The river merges with the ocean, but if one takes sweet water from the river and places it in a sealed plastic bag and places that sealed bag in the ocean, there is no mixing of that water with the ocean. Such a condition could be compared to one's state before coming here, but after coming here it is as though the sweet water were not held separate from the ocean but were merged and mixed with the ocean. This is the mixing stage, here. Swami is the servant of all, which He enjoys much more than being a master.

H: What is the meaning of the word 'Dharma'?

Sai: The word 'Dharma' does not mean duty. In duty there is no freedom; in reason there is freedom; and in religious obligation there is the union between duty and reason. 'Dharma,' then, refers to religious obligation and in that word are the concepts of both duty and reason.

Visitor: There is a difficulty that arises in doing honor to two different aspects of the Lord. For example, Mother in Sri Aurobindo's ashram, and Swamiji here.

Sai: There are two ways; one in which the Divine is seen everywhere, and there is then no conflict whatsoever; and the other way in which one feels strong devotion to one single

15

person and is happy in that devotion. In the latter case, one should hold strictly to that guru and have nothing to do with other gurus. When one works at a task one needs to give that task full attention and concentration and cannot be thinking of the Lord while doing that task. But the principle involved is the attitude of dedicating everything to the Lord and not doing work because of the fruit to be gained from that work but, on the contrary, doing the work because it is one's duty to do it very well.

[A Visitor: Can I wear shorts while here at the ashram?
Sai: No. That should not be.]

Sai: In spiritual life, the fastest progress is made when the boat sails with the wind, and if the boat has to sail against the wind, progress is slower.

A Visitor: Well, Swami, the trouble is to determine which way the wind is blowing.

Sai: That is really very simple. With practice, a driver of a car learns to be so skilful at driving that a wide boulevard or a narrow road makes no difference to him, he drives both with equal confidence. In the same way, a guru is necessary in order to learn how to take advantage of the wind in the sea of the spirit. The trouble is that nowadays it is very difficult to find a guru. As soon as a person puts on a yellow robe he considers himself a guru and wants to teach people. The best way to determine whether or not a guru is genuine is if his words are full of wisdom and if in his life he practices and is the same as his words. If the guru speaks only words of wisdom—and this is an age where people speak wisdom without being wise—the words of wisdom will produce no result whatsoever and are useless.

The best guru today is God. In the spiritual world, the guru is a doctor who takes the temperature of the aspirant and from the temperature is able to gauge his condition and what is best for him. But if the guru himself has a temperature, then the temperature of the aspirant would be distorted by the temperature of the guru. So the best guru today is God.

A Visitor: Swami, one hears talk of mantras.

Sai: Just the repetition of a mantrum is of no value, but if the mantrum is chanted with full knowledge of its significance, it has a great effect.

A Visitor: How can we improve memory?

Sai: There is not much use thinking about the past, because it is gone. Trying to memorize is not of much value. We will naturally remember that in which we are interested. A small story: Arjuna was 85 years old, a middle-aged man. In those days people lived much longer. Arjuna said, 'Lord, how is it that you can remember all the past lives, and I cannot?' Krishna replied, 'Well, ten years ago on the third day of the month, what were you doing?' Arjuna said, 'I do not know.' Then Krishna said, 'Well, you were alive then.' Arjuna replied, 'Yes, I was alive.'

Krishna then said, 'Look back, Arjuna, 60 years to the day you were married, do you remember that?' 'Oh, yes,' replied Arjuna, 'I remember that.' 'Then, look further back, Arjuna, to the day you met your guru and were taught the martial arts. Do you remember?' 'Yes,' replied Arjuna, 'I remember.' Then Krishna said, 'It is obvious that men remember that in which they are interested, that in which they are sufficiently intense to cause them to remember the incident. But that in which they are not intensely interested, they do not bother remembering. Now, you do not remember 20 years back, but you know you were alive then, therefore the memory is there, but you cannot recall it. Now, I remember everything, Arjuna, because I am interested in everything.'

A Visitor (carrying a professional camera): Can I take your picture now?

Sai (in English): How many are here? Two, three, four, five, six, seven, eight, nine, ten . . . twelve.

A Visitor: Twelve disciples.

Sai: This is my camera. (Swami opens His hand and there are 12 small pictures of Himself. Much exclamation from the group.) Keep them in your purse. See, twelve! Full address also!

17

Address here in India. No camera, no film, no flash. A visiting card. Puttaparthi is the address. (Sai opens a silver box and starts preparing leaves.)

Visitor: What is that?

Sai (in English): That is the nut. This is the leaf. See, the leaves, and this is the betel. This is not a bad habit. If it were a bad habit, Swami would not chew it. The leaves, their juice, purifies the blood. The nut digests. Here, even with the little puppies, they mix the nut and give it for digestion. And the other thing that is put in is calcium. The three mixed make the red color. This is Indian. (The foregoing was said in a joking voice, accompanied by much merriment from the foreign visitors.)

A Visitor: The pictures that people take of Swami and then produce for sale are not good pictures. They do not do justice to Swami. Swami is perfect and everything around Him should be perfect.

Sai: Some may like one thing and others may not like that thing. The liking and disliking is not in the object, but in our minds. If a person judges from appearance, then it indicates a lack of depth. First one should know Swami, and then make a judgment.

A Visitor: But Swami is beautiful and the pictures make Him ugly.

Sai: Love is the beauty.

Translator: Swami says that because we love Him we see the beauty. So whoever wants to will come to Him. You need not get upset because of pictures.

Sai: Johnson—you know, Johnson the English writer and scholar—he had an ugly wife, but he loved her very much. A friend said, 'Your wife looks old and made up.' She did not look young and beautiful. Friends thought she looked old and made up. But he thought her beautiful. Love is blind.

A Visitor: Master, yesterday you said this is ego and that is God. Does this being here help?

Sai: Oh, yes. When you make friendship with God, then all the three gunas go away from you. This ego and anger and

18

jealousy. Scientifically also, the blood goes to the top and then circulates back. When it goes there and turns, there is speed; it goes faster. This is a most important point in life.

A Visitor: How does one get devotion to God?

Sai: Confidence is necessary. Food is the start. The body is made from food. Without health, it is very hard to do anything. The stomach is of four parts: ¼ part air, ¼ part food, and ½ part water. Too much food is taken nowadays; there is no room for water. In India, rice and wheat are standard. They are all right if taken in moderation. But people eat too much and get dull. Too much food results in dullness of mind. Food in moderation does not result in sickness. Swami travels to various parts of India and does not get sick from food. Swami becomes sick only when taking on the sickness of a devotee. Otherwise, never. Too much milk is bad. It is rajasic.

Visitor: Sai Baba, this is for me, this is not for anybody, just for myself—my food. Meat is important. Meat is my food.

Sai: Food is important for the body. Even for being born, food is the reason. Mother and father have been nourished with food and they then give birth to a child. The parents have grown up on food. The whole body is a food bundle. The type of food you eat, that kind of thoughts will come to your mind. If you have satwic food, there will be a satwic effect. Fruit and milk—everything that is cool and not hot like strong onions. Meat gives the blood its effect, like passion and similar qualities. Dirty thoughts come with fish. Although fish is always in water, it has a bad smell.

A Visitor: How about lamb?

Sai: Meat is all right for those who concentrate on the body and want to have strength, but for spiritual aspirants it is not good.

A Visitor: But the proteins that come from meat?

Sai: Yes, with meat the body will get the proteins, but mental proteins will not be there. If you are keen on spiritual life, eating meat is not worthwhile; but if you are keen on worldly life, it is all right. There is another spiritual reason.

When you kill an animal you give him suffering, pain, harm. God is in every creature, so how can you give such pain? Sometimes when someone beats a dog he cries, he feels so much pain. How much more pain then in killing. Animals did not come for the purpose of supplying food to human beings. They came to work out their own life in the world. When a human being is dead, the foxes and other animals may eat, but we have not come to provide food for those that eat the human body; we have not come for that purpose. Similarly, man eats the animal, but the animal has not come to provide man with food. But we have taken to eating meat as a habit.

A Visitor: But we take milk, which is animal.

Sai: Anything that comes from the cow, a little milk, butter, cheese, is all right for the spiritual aspirant. There is no harm to the cow, and it is of benefit to take it. In Dwapara Yuga, before Kali Yuga, 5680 years back, milk came into favor. Eleven thousand years is the full length of the Kali Yuga.

A Visitor: Does Kali Yuga still continue?

Sai: Yes.

Visitor: Because in America several books say Kali Yuga has ended and another is in force.

Sai: No. Before the Kali Yuga ends, there is a space in between. The situation is similar to the motion of a fan. When the fan is started there is an interval before it picks up speed, and when the switch is turned off, the fan continues to run for a time. The world is also turning round like the fan. Even if the Kali Yuga stops, it still has a few more revolutions to go before the final ending. The situation is somewhat as found with a string of light poles. There is a distance of about a furlong between each pole. The light from a pole extends about half way to the next pole and at some point the light of the next pole is faintly there also. There are four Yugas. The sequence is circular, and when the last is finished, the whole cycle starts all over again. Kali Yuga still has 5,320 years before ending.

A Visitor: How does Kali Yuga fit into the astrological signs?

20

Sai: The predictions made in astrology are somewhat different from each other in their readings, and this implies some error. It is difficult to pinpoint time factors precisely, and this leads to errors. Astrology is able to view the stars from only one angle of vision; the stars are not seen totally and this is a source of error. Everything changes. People change and so also do the stars. Astrologers do not take these changes into account and this is a source of error. Astrologers do not know their science perfectly and this leads to errors. Astrologers are not living lives of great purity and for this reason spiritual help is not fully within their reach, and this leads to errors. With all these errors, astrology cannot be relied on and it is not worth bothering with.

A Visitor: What should be done for my leg? It is still swollen and hurts.

Sai: Do not move around and climb on the hills. Take rest.

Visitor: Oh. When I climbed to that tree on the hill, I did not realize.

Sai: You must rest and take care of the body. Body is like a boat. Life is like a river. On this side is the world. On the other side is God. And so, to reach the other side, that is, to reach God, you must maintain this boat carefully. You keep the boat for any length of time in the water; there is no danger. But if the water comes into the boat, then there is danger. You can remain in the world for any number of years, but don't let the world take hold. Don't let the world take hold of the inside world. There is the example of the lotus. Deep down in the mud it stays. It comes up to the light, and it can't stay without water because it would die. But it does not get mixed up either with the mud or the water. You have seen the lotus; even if the water comes it just goes off again. Now, when they talk of God, they always say 'the lotus eyes, the lotus feet' because of this inner significance.

Sai (to a Visitor): If you had fashionable earrings would you wear them?

Visitor: Oh, yes. (Sai moves His hand and there appears a set of golden, jewelled earrings which he gives to the visitor.)

Sai: See, they are fashionable, but the value is not high. (Sai now moves over to where the visitor is sitting and himself places the earrings on her ears. Much exclamation from the individuals in the group.)

A Visitor (who is somewhat bald): Swami, can you grow hair?

(Sai starts to make some comment, but the visitor interrupts.)

Visitor: No, just a joke, Swami.

Translator: Swami can do anything. Swami says that he gives earrings to the lady to bring her joy. The more joy, the more the disease will go.

Sai: That is the medicine for her. Joy is the medicine.

Visitor: I wanted to go to the hill to see the Kalpataru Tree.

Sai: This is the Kalpataru Tree. Swami is the Kalpataru Tree. Anything you want, Swami is able to give. If you want anything, here is the tree. This is the gold shop also, and the camera shop! (Much merriment from the group.)

A Visitor: Swami's gifts are beautiful, but what if one only wants peace of mind?

Sai: Only thoughts of God and intense love for Him bring peace. As worldly thoughts diminish, thoughts of God increase. Normally, the mind desires these worldly things all the time. As the desires are cut out one by one, the peace becomes stronger. You weave the threads and there is the cloth. If the threads are removed, there is no longer cloth. When there are Godly thoughts, there is peace of mind. Swami cannot give peace of mind, one has to work for it. We do meditation, spiritual practices in this temporary body. Though this body is temporary, you have to use temporary things to realize the truth.

Visitor: But I wanted to know about peace.

Sai: Yes. If the desires are cut off one by one, then there is peace. When the desires go one by one, then there is die-mind. Then there is peace of mind. Swami cannot give peace of mind; you must work for it yourselves. First, stop the questioning and ask, 'Who am I?' This is my body, my mind, my intelligence. But who is this 'my'? Who is it that claims the ownership of that which is declared to be 'mine'? 'My,' 'My' indicates ownership. That 'my' is the life. As long as the life is in the body, there is this connection between the 'my' and the intellect—'my' body, 'my' house, 'my' land. But the moment you remove the life from the body, there is no 'my' or sense of possession.

Life is God. 'Who am I?' The answer is 'I am God.' The body comes and goes, but the Atma is permanent. The body has birth and death, but the spirit does not have any of these. You reach the stage where you say, 'I am God,' but even there, there is duality, 'God and I.' That is not the full truth.

When we breathe, the breath makes the sound of 'So-Hum,' 'He am I.' There is still the body consciousness, the 'I.' But in deep sleep, the declaration of 'He' and 'I' falls away and only 'O' and 'M' remain: 'Om.' There is only the One.

H: One understands this and has for some time, but when does intellectual comprehension change to reality?

Sai: It will become reality only when you practice it intensely. You read so much. You do not have to practice all that you read. Take one or two things to practice and then it will become a reality to you. When you go to the hospital, there are so many medicines. You do not have to take all the medicines; just the ones that are needed for your malady. You do not have to eat all the medicines. Whatever kind of spiritual practices you sincerely want to do, you just take that medicine; do not collect all the other things. Because too much of this book-knowledge just leads to doubts and confusion. You get too many doubts asking what is this and what is that, and you waste a lot of time in this conflict.

H: What does the supreme spiritual Doctor say is the correct medicine for me?

Sai: Meditation. For in meditation you first get sense control. And yoga will help you with the body. And when the mind is steady, concentration will come automatically. When you get such concentration, then you get peace of mind.

End of Interview

III

H: Swami says that 'All is done by the Lord, and not by you.' But, the world over, there is the concept that man is responsible for his own actions.

Sai: You are God. As long as you are being human, there may be such thoughts.

H: 'As long as you are being human.' Does that imply the human state as an act of one's will?

Sai: Not an act of will. Just a matter of being confused. It is a delusion. You come here with doubts. Swami knows that, so he gives you a chance to ask. If a Jnani comes, a man with direct experience of the divine, Swami does not ask him what are his doubts. The fact that you have questions is evidence that you are on the worldly level. Baba's teaching will vary according to the level of the person. A teacher in a school may at the same time be a renowned Vedic scholar, but when teaching a child to read, he can only say, 'This letter is 'A.' This letter is 'B' ' and so on. Mother may feed one child at the breast, give soft food to another, tell the cook to serve food to another, and tell the eldest to serve himself. But though her treatment of each child may be different, her love is equal for all. There are four different stages in which man finds himself, and God gives different but appropriate help to each: first are those persons who are in distress, second are those desiring prosperity, third are those engaged in enquiry as to what is truth, and fourth are the wise ones. At present, in you, there is a mixture of conscious and subconscious. For this reason there is confusion and doubt, in the unconscious state there is no doubt, there is decision; in this state there is no body and no mind, although there may be visions. There is still another state beyond the super-conscious. This is Divine consciousness where God alone is. In the super-conscious state there is still a very slight tinge of duality, of giver and receiver. In the ordinary state there are the three: giver, gift and receiver. In divine consciousness there is the giver only. Really, all other than the One is false. Even sadhana. Here a doubt may arise: how can sadhana, something false, result in something other than false? It is like this; a dream is unreal, but the dream may become so strong, so terrifying, that because of the dream one awakens. It is likewise with sadhana. For sadhana to become so strong that from it one awakens to reality, the sadhana must be persistent into the super-conscious level where both body and mind are transcended. It is from the deep transcendent state that Truth blazes forth.

H: One hears about various paths to self-realization. What does this mean?

Sai: There are three paths. There is that of devotion; the guru guides and all is left to the guru to perform. Then, there is the perception that God is Omnipresent; the future comes up to the present and the past falls away from the present. God is omnipresent; so the present is God; this is knowledge. Then there is surrender to God. But surrender does not mean just doing all actions in His name. Surrender to God is when the entire Universe is known as His body. Surrender is when doer, deed, and object are all God. It cannot be forced. It comes naturally. Faith is the foundation; surrender is the peak.

H: Of the many 'roads' to self-realization, what is the short cut?

Sai: The short cut is this way: the name of God is the seed; love is the water by which the crop grows, discipline is the fence which protects the growing crop; the field in which the crop is grown is the spiritual heart; the crop when it comes to harvest, is Bliss.

H: Why should one attempt to gain self-realization when one is always self-realized?

Sai: As of now, there is a mixture in the mind of sensory identification. The mind is not fully one-pointed.

H: Swami, time is needed for the plane to arrive in India, but why is time needed for self-realization? Is not an immediate awakening possible, entirely apart from time?

Sai: Immediate awakening apart from time? Yes, it is possible. If faith is full and perfect, then Grace comes fully at that very moment—just as the sound and the bullet occur at the same moment.

H: But, Swami, one believes that he does have full faith. Therefore, there must be self-deception.

Sai: As long as one thinks he has faith, he does not. Just as when one knows that he is meditating, he is not meditating. Only when meditation is automatic, all day long, is there meditation. Full faith is reached by sadhana, just as Bombay is reached by approaching it.

H: Sadhana, as it is described, seems wrong, because it is a conscious effort aimed at getting a reward. It seems to me that sadhana is real only when it is spontaneous. That is, when one naturally loves God, then he cannot help but love God, and he cannot help but make enquiry.

Sai: It is as you say, but you have not experienced that spontaneous love of God; it is still just an idea. You have a conviction that love of God exists naturally in you. That conviction is the result of many lives of spiritual practice.

A Visitor: What is the correct sadhana for retired people?

Sai: Meditation morning and evening. Spend the days in good work.

A Visitor: What is the sadhana appropriate to ladies?

Sai: Ladies have the duty of house, children and husband. They are very busy. Meditation morning and evening can be done. During the day, all work that previously was done for others should now be done as worship of God. That is the best sadhana for ladies.

26

IV

H: This morning in the taxi from the airport, even the driver had a marvelous experience of Swami's leelas. And, the Bombay airport officers told other miraculous stories about happenings in their homes.

Sai: Leelas are occurring throughout India in tens of millions of homes. Swami keeps His hand down so that publicity about the leelas will not spread. The rulers of the country know, but they keep it quiet. If the facts were to have publicity, millions would converge on Swami. The Government would surround Him with security guards, and devotees could not get close to Him. The time is not ready.

H: In the future, when millions of people are crowding around Swami, will our present chance of being close by be gone?

Sai: Not at all. If Baba is pleased with a person, he may still be close. That is Baba's will.

H: Only a relative few are fortunate enough to see Swami and appreciate that it is God come within our vision.

Sai: One sees a plane in the sky. He cannot see the pilot, but he knows there is a pilot. To see the pilot, he must buy a ticket. The Universe also has a Pilot. He is God. To see Him, the ticket is His grace. This can be won by sadhana of the various types. Underlying all sadhana is love. The reality of all sadhana is love. Without love, no sadhana has any value. To win God's grace, faith is necessary. Without love, there cannot be faith. That love is in the heart and arises spontaneously therefrom. Love is God. That love which fills the heart is Swami, who is the resident of the heart.

H: What is 100 percent faith in God?

Sai: One hundred percent faith arises from the Atma. Full faith is even, unchanging. Through pain and sorrow, faith in God remains full. Milk may be compared to life. In the whey there is no oil. Butter has some remains of water—this is the good and the bad—the butter the good tendencies, the water the bad. When the butter is boiled, at a certain stage there is a bad smell. This is the remaining impurities being boiled away. But have faith and keep on during that period. Then the pure ghee is left. That pure ghee is wisdom. The end of wisdom is freedom.

V

H: Swami, something has happened here. Water is around this box. These saris will get wet. (Swami removed the cover of the box and those of us who were standing there could see that the edges of the saris were wet. The cardboard box with four saris in it was sitting on a table at the Dharmakshetra in Bombay. Swami had selected 96 saris for distribution to some lady volunteers, and of the 100 brought for His inspection, four were replaced in the box to be returned later to the merchant. The table was not close to any source of water, and Hislop, several other men, and Swami had been standing there from the time the saris were examined one by one, by Swami.)

Sai: The saris are weeping because Swami has rejected them. Now I will take them.

H: Swami! How could that be? Does Swami say that inanimate objects have injured feelings and can weep?

Sai: Inanimate objects are also capable of feeling joy and grief. When the bridge towards Lanka was built by the monkeys so that Rama could march to Ravana's kingdom where Sita was held captive, one last mountain peak was carried to the bridge site. But it was too late. There was no need for it. At this circumstance the mountain shed tears of anguish, and news of this was quickly taken to Rama. His compassion was great, and He sent word that the mountain should no longer sorrow, that He would surely use it on a future occasion. In the Avathara of Krishna, it was this very mountain peak, the Govardhana Peak, which the youth, Krishna, lifted on His finger to shelter the cowherds of Gokul from Indra's deluge of rain.

H: Swami! This great drama of Rama and Krishna and the

mountain peak has been recapitulated here in Bombay on this day before our very eyes. The saris came and could not be used. They wept tears of anguish; and in His compassion Swami relented, and the rejected saris will be used, although not for the original purpose of making gifts to the volunteers. (Mrs. Hislop and three other ladies were given the rejected saris.) It is the self-same drama of ancient days played again on this day.

Sai: Yes. And it is also the self-same Rama and the self-same Krishna who is here this day.

VI

A Visitor: One sees oneself in a mirror. As one moves away from the mirror, the image becomes smaller and smaller. I sit here and look at Hislop. The further away I move, the smaller Hislop becomes. But Hislop is not smaller; he has not changed. Therefore, I cannot be looking at Hislop. But Hislop is certainly there. So what did I see when I thought I was seeing Hislop? And if Hislop is not that which I see, then what is Hislop? Do I, in some way or other, see a reflection of Hislop?

Sai: It is indeed true that you do not see Hislop. You see a reflection of Hislop, the reflection exhibits that particular form and characteristics. Then what is Hislop? Hislop is God. The image, the form is not God, but all forms together, the totality of all forms can be taken as God. God is the reality behind the form. The world is there, but its reality is not seen. The reality is God. One may see the reality, that the truth behind every form is God. Once this perception arises, it is never lost. Although one sees the forms, he is always aware of the truth, the reality.

Visitor: There is an experience that I have. The Scriptures name it Nirvikalpa Samadhi; pure consciousness, consciousness without any object. After having had experience of that state of being, I lose it. Can one do anything to stem that loss?

Sai: It is like this. When rain leaves the clouds, it is pure, but becomes contaminated when it reaches the ground. That water may be purified by some technique, but it cannot be equated with the purity of the rain. In like fashion, you lose the Nirvikalpa Samadhi state when duty calls you to your work. Sadhana will purify that worldly life, but that purified life is not the same as Nirvikalpa Samadhi.

Visitor: Should I leave my work?

Sai: No. Just do the work; not for your employers, but for God.

Visitor: I will try to apply this lesson when I return to my home and my work.

VII

(A group of farmers, from whom Swami had purchased a parcel of land adjoining the college, came with a bag to carry away the purchase money. But Swami gave them six times as much money as had been agreed upon for the purchase. The larger sum was also larger in bulk and would not fit into the bag which the farmers had brought with them. The farmers could not understand why they were given so much money.)

Farmer: Lord, how can we possibly eat your money? Take it back.

Sai: No. The extra rupees are to get started in some business. For now that the land is sold, how will you manage? Everyone should work and earn their living.

VIII

Sai: The ten rupee note tells you that it has seen many faces and will see many more. Money comes to your hand, but does not stay; whereas morality comes and stays. Money comes and goes; morality comes and grows. With many people, they are quite agreeable misusing money for self-indulgence, for bad action, but if the possibility comes up to use the money for a good purpose, they at once become extremely cautious and reluctant and bring up many objections.

IX

H: Swami, on the road to Simla, drivers were very reckless in trying to stay close behind Swami's car. At one moment, our car, which was going at a high speed, swerved to miss another car and was about to run down a policeman at the side of the road. It seemed sure there was neither time nor space to avoid striking him, but at the last second only his uniform was brushed by the car and he was not harmed. Surely, it must be Swami who is driving every devotee's car, is it not?

Sai: No. It is the driver's responsibility. He must exercise caution and responsibility. It is only at the moment of an accident that Swami takes over the situation.

H: Why does Swami conduct a marriage ceremony for older people who are long married?

Sai: In India, at age 60, people have a second marriage as rebirth of the marriage into spiritual life directed to God and not concerned with the senses. Prior to age 60, the couple were entitled to enjoy the fruits of the senses. At the age of 70, seven also has a significance. There are seven great rishis and at age 70 a person should be merged with these saints. At age 80, there are eight Deities reigning over the directions. At age 90, there are nine special planets, and we should be merged with them. At age 100, one should be master of the five working organs, and the five sense organs, and should be merged with God. The five working organs are talking, taking, walking, rejecting (excrement), and eating. The five sense organs are hearing, touch, sight, taste and smell.

An Indian Visitor: These Hindu rites, is there anything to them?

Sai: We owe debts of gratitude, and this gratitude must be

31

expressed at the appropriate time, and in such a way as will enable the message to be delivered. Our gratitude is due to the two parents, guru, God, nature, and the sages. If a letter is sent correctly addressed, it will reach its destination, and one need not know about, or worry about the transit terminals through which the letter passes en route. In the case of the parents, their bodies have died, but the Atma has suffered no change. The correct address for the expression of gratitude is provided by the mantra used in the ceremony. Mantras are very powerful, and in olden days they were relied upon. Nowadays machines are relied upon. The experts in mantras were called saints. The experts in machines are called scientists.

(A visiting scientist raised a doubt about science vs. what Swami says.)

Sai: Science is highly fragmentary, and its approach to reality is through Maya, and this is a highly dangerous procedure. Science does not even know the truth of chemistry and physics. Each ten years or so, the old truths are discarded or modified because of research results. So, when man tries to compare science and the spiritual world of Baba, he is comparing a science whose finality is not known, to spiritual truth of which he is also ignorant. Science is from the senses downward. Spirit is from the senses upward. Science does not even know of the great holes in the sun through which winds rush to regulate the temperature. Science is just hit and miss. For one to really know, he must have the total, over-all knowledge of Baba.

H: Is there a reliable English translation of the Vedas?

Sai: The Vedas come from certain fundamental sounds and their variations. The slightest modification of the sound changes the meaning of what is said. No written language is able to represent all of the Vedic sounds. It is impossible to write many of the words. The Vedas are God's breath and can be transmitted from person to person only by voice. In all of India there are only a handful of people who can recite the Vedas correctly. Some attempts have been made in recent years to write the Vedas and print them in books. The effort is wasted.

X

Sai: The Universe is a globe. Earth and all beings are smaller globes within that. The whole universe is held in Baba's hand.

XI

Sai: Forget the world. Give up the Jiva. Reach God. Of the various sadhanas, repetition of the name of God is the most effective. If that is not done, Karma is next best. If no sadhana is done, then love of God is enough. With love of God no discipline or practice is necessary. Love of God is enough.

XII

H: Why does Baba have regular schools? Why does he not have religious schools?

Sai: Religious schools would appeal only to the religious, whereas Baba's task is to raise the general public into devotion and spiritual life. One aspect of Baba's task is to reform education, and if that were impossible He would not have come. Now, having come, be assured the task will be accomplished. But not as fast as impatient humans would like. By an intensive TV campaign, a change could be made fast, but it would be only temporary. God sees differently than man, and He knows that to start early, drive slowly, reach safely is correct. The change that Baba is bringing about may be through slow methods, such as His colleges, but the methods will be effective.

H: What should we do about young people to correct their character and behavior?

Sai: A child is bound to touch a hot lamp until once burned. Young people are without balance. Also, they want immediate results. For example: yesterday there was a marriage here. The young man wanted a son at once; he did not wish to wait for nine months. A guru (so-called) comes into view, and the young people flock to him, hoping for quick self-realization. But, once disappointed, they turn away and, in the process, gain some caution and patience. A small story: A young man of very poor parents graduated B.A., mainly because the teachers were fed up with his many failures at the exams. His parents were now proud and said, 'We will find you a wife.' The boy replied, 'I will take only a B.A. girl, for I am a B.A.' Mother said, 'We cannot afford servants for a girl who will come from her room at 9 a.m. We need a wife to help with the housework.' The son replied, 'It is my needs that matter, not yours. Do as I wish or I will leave.' The parents capitulated and secured the desired wife. The boy told friends, 'I am now happiness itself.' Three days later he said to his wife, 'My dear, arise now and make me coffee.' She replied, 'My dear, I am B.A. same as you. Please arise and get coffee for me!' Now the boy proclaimed to all that life had become black and all was unhappiness to total misery. These behaviors of the young are typical because they have not been taught to respect and revere their parents. Their behavior in the spiritual direction is similar. How can there be any spiritual light until the inside is clean? And inside work is quiet inquiry and discrimination. After the inside is clean, outward disciplines may have some value.

H: Young people nowadays ask how they can respect their parents, when the parents engage in wrong actions.

Sai: The young people do not realize the worry of the parents. No matter how faulty the parents, they wish only the best for their children. At the very least, the children can honor this and also realize the sacrifice, care, and love given to the child to keep it alive and give it a chance for life. These factors must be appreciated and honored even though the parents have faults. Only by honoring the parents will the children's children do honor to them. A clear case of action and reaction.

H: Swami, if the parent says one thing and the guru says another, to which order should the child give preference?

Sai: The parents who give the body come before God.

H: Parents come before God, Swami? That is surprising.

Sai: For people in the worldly sphere, that is true. For young people leading a pure spiritual life, God comes first of all.

H: Swami, these young college students who are in Swami's college here have a first-class external education–highest examination scores and so on. They are also building an inner character of strong morality. Will not these students become the leaders of India? Will not their fine education get them positions and their strong morality sustain them?

Sai: That is the purpose of Swami's college.

H: Then in 20 or 30 years we should look for a great change in the Indian nation.

Sai: Twenty years? In ten years.

H: But Swami, in 10 years they are still in their late twenties. People come to power in the late thirties, in their 40's and 50's.

Sai: In India people reach positions of power and influence earlier in life. Even now there are a number of examples throughout the nation.

H: Do these students realize their destiny and the great responsibility to the world that they will carry?

Sai: The students say that when they grow up they will do as Sai wills. As positions open in every area of the Indian society, these young men will occupy the positions. Wherever they go they will influence and change the society for the better. Corruption and such problems will sharply diminish. Their influence cannot but express itself. Right now, 80 percent of the parents of the students have had their lives changed because they observe the effect of Sai on the characters of their children. The parents are content. They say they will not interfere and that their children should follow the guidance of Sai.

Sai: (pointing to a young student from Hong Kong) This boy will speak tomorrow. (A number of students were gathered around the door of Swami's dining room, as He was having His evening meal.)

H (to the student): Have you prepared your speech?

Student: Swami is my voice. What He says will form into words in my mouth and will be spoken.

H: You are saying that you make no speech preparation whatsoever? Surely the first idea must be in your mind so you can get started. Tell me what you have in mind to say.

Student: I do not make ideas. Only by the prompting of Bhagavan, who resides in my heart, do ideas come to mind. He is God and there is nothing else but him.

Sai (to student): Speak now.

Student: Swami's being is pure beauty. His eyes tell me to watch my thoughts, watch my action, watch my words, watch my heart. His smile is like a beautiful rose whose fragrance fills the garden of my life.

Sai (to student): How do you know Swami is God?

Student: (is silent).

Sai (to Hislop): Go ahead. Ask him some questions.

H: How does one know that Swami is God? It is not very clear.

Student: Swami gives a person the power to know Him.

H: How do you mean?

Student: When the three gunas are in balance, Satwic, Rajas and Tamas—when those three qualities or characteristics are in balance with each other so that the person is balanced, when that happens by means of discipline, devotion and duty, then Swami is pleased to give the power to know that He is God.

H: When does that happen? At an early age, or later on?

Student: Age is not the important factor. The balance of one's nature is the important thing and this is by the practice of duty, devotion and discipline.

H: What is the destiny of man?

Student: His destiny is to realize that he is the embodiment of God.

H: Do girls have this same destiny?

Student: There may be some difference, but really both are the same. When Swami is at the girl's College at Anantapur, the boys here at the Brindavan College realize that He is omnipresent and that He is still here even though He is at Anantapur. They know that if their devotion is strong enough, He will come back to Brindavan. The girls are the same. They know that Swami is omnipresent and that if their devotion is strong enough, He will visit Anantapur College in His physical person.

H: What is your career? What are you going to do in life?

Student: I will do that which Swami tells me to do.

H: No plan to do anything? No wish to do this kind of work or that kind of work?

Student: When the correct plan comes, Swami will guide me into the work that is my correct duty in the world. Just as He has guided these older boys standing there who have now taken up careers in the University.

H: This is a strange idea to people in the world. The world over, young men arrive at their own decision as to a career, and then try for success in that career by applying their full energy.

Student: They did not know about their career until some inner prompting told them. Until that time they did not know. The same for yourself. Until Swami told you to be President of the American Sai organization, you did not know about that.

H: That is for sure! I certainly had no such wish or idea prior to Swami saying. But you are so sure that Swami is God. Many people come here and go away not believing that. Their circumstances and early influences have bent them another way and so they are not able to see Swami as you do. How about them?

Student: Some trees grow up straight towards the sky, some are bent and twisted by weather and storm. It does not really matter. Even the most twisted person will come to know Swami is God.

H: How can you say that? How will that happen?

Student: It cannot do other than happen. Swami, as God, is the resident of each person's heart and the irresistible strength of this fact cannot but eventually make itself known.

H: You are so sure about it. But you are just a boy, just starting to experience life. Suppose a full grown, widely experienced man comes to you and says, 'I tell you that Swami is just a man, an extraordinarily intelligent and powerful man.' What would you say?

Student: Swami has taught us not to rely on the experience of another person but to trust in our own experience. My experience is that Swami is God, and your experience is not mine.

H: When you go out into the world, very likely you will get married. How will you relate to your wife?

Student: Swami will have given me the wife. Swami is my spiritual father and mother, and in the real sense I am born of Him. He is God, and my wife is not different from Him. He is in her heart also. So I will regard my wife as mother, sister, and God.

H: Well, I have heard that Mother and Father are to be regarded as God. But this is the first time I have heard that one's wife is to be regarded as God. I believe you are going to face some problems in this matter.

Sai (to Hislop in Telugu via another student): Ask him what he will do if his wife says he cannot come to Puttaparthi?

H: You know, sometimes a wife develops a very strong personality and takes command of the family. Suppose such a wife says to you, 'You do not go to Puttaparthi.'

Student: I would not mind. You must know that a diamond has several faces. The largest face, with the most reflective power, represents God. But each smaller facet is of the same diamond. My wife, who represents a smaller facet of the diamond is also God. And my home is Puttaparthi. So I would be content with my Puttaparthi, with God in command.

H: You say God is the diamond and that the brilliance of the largest facet represents Him. Suppose Swami says 'Come to Puttaparthi,' and your wife says, 'Do not go.'

Student: It is God that I obey, not the wife as such. I would go to Puttaparthi.

Sai (in another aside to Hislop): Ask him what if his wife says she would leave him.

H: The wife is one body and mind, Swami is another. The wife has her independent viewpoint. You tell her, 'I will go to Puttaparthi. You may stay here.' But your wife says to you, 'You will not find me when you return. I will leave you.'

Student: Such a wife is not my wife. I would go to Puttaparthi. She may act according to her own decision.

Sai: Ask the boys some questions. (The college boys were outside in the compound circled around Sai.)

H: (to student) What do you want?

Student: I want Swami.

H: I mean after you graduate and go out into life.

Student: I want Swami.

H: Who is Swami?

Student: He is Love. He is God.

H: Where is Swami?

Student: In my heart.

H: If Swami is in your heart then you already have Swami. What do you want to do in life? Doctor? Lawyer? Prime Minister?

Student: I will do as Swami tells me to do.

H: Who is Hislop?

Student: He is Swami.

H: Then why do you not say, 'I want Hislop?'

Student: Hislop is a small portion of Swami. Whereas Swami is God in full.

Sai: (laughing) Hislop is a big tall man, whereas Swami is the small one, about 5 feet tall.

H: How do you know that Swami is God?

Student: I see that He is God.

H: But you see Swami's body. How do you see Him as God?

Student: We have confidence that He is God.

H: Where is God?

Student: God is everywhere.

H: When you look at that tree, what do you see?

Student: I see God.

H: How does this faith arise that God is everywhere?

Student: There is some small experience of Swami; then there is faith.

Sai: No. Faith comes first and then experience. Students must not only know the answers to questions. The answers must be in the conduct of their lives, and on this basis they must teach others. Faith is natural to each person. Each person has some faith in himself, some confidence in himself. And the core of his being, of himself, is Atma. From this is the foundation of faith in himself. A small example: One does not remember his birth and Mother tells him the date. He does not know by himself, but through faith he accepts what mother says. Father may not have been present at that event, but Mother gave birth. She does not need to ask anyone. Some reflection will indicate that for the coming into being of the universe there must also be a basis. God is that basis. He knows. He need not ask anyone. In that subtle area, beyond body and intellect, only faith can exist. Faith is natural with each person, and so also is love. Love is directed to various objects and to various persons, but love of God is the essential factor. Looking at that tree we note that the many branches, leaves and twigs have one trunk as the factor common to all of them. The trunk in turn relies on the roots. To try to water each leaf and each branch would take much time and the water would be wasted. But if we direct all the water to the roots of the tree, then each branch and leaf and twig will naturally receive moisture in the way that is best for it. As it is now, people say they love friends, and relatives but do not love God. God is the basis of all individuals. He is the root from which all have their being. It is best to love God first and to love Him with all one's heart. Then your love will naturally include the various individuals.

H: Swami, when the college boys give speeches they say that Swami gives them the words. Can this be correct?

Sai: Sai gives them confidence. With confidence the words arise automatically.

Sai (to a college boy): What do you want when you finish college?

Student: I want only to merge with Swami.

Sai: Now, the Avathar has taken a body to revive Dharma. He is here, engaged in that. So what is all this talk of immortality and merging? Your whole life is before you. First, find out what is the purpose of this life. If God Himself is here to foster Dharma, and you engage yourself in the same task, then you are worshipping Him. Then you are near and dear to Him, for you are serving Him, His devotees, and yourself.

XIII

H: (at Prasanthi Nilayam) Swami, what is that new construction on the other side of the sheds?

Sai: That is an oil pressing plant. Farmers in this area can bring their groundnuts and press out the oil free of charge.

H: I had heard that Swami was making a cottage industry for the villagers in these large sheds, but I did not know about the farmers.

Sai: The Gokulam is also a model dairy to show the farmers. The cottage industry is to free the villagers from their poverty by showing them how to work and have an income from work.

H: That large shed beside the new High School that Swami is building, what is that for?

Sai: There the students may learn skills to help them in a practical way; how to fix machines, carpentry, electricity, plumbing, construction of buildings, and so on.

H: Will that be a feature of all the schools that Sai builds?

Sai: Yes. Girls will learn sewing and household skills.

XIV

H: Is not praying to God the same as begging?

Sai: To beg from an equal puts you down and him up. But when you ask God, you rise up to His level. You must ask God. To ask God is perfectly all right. It is not begging.

H: But I had thought that since God knows each problem, that if it was appropriate to remedy the trouble God would do so without being asked.

Sai: Important answer! No. It is your duty to ask God. Words must be said, and the words must correspond to the thought. The thought must be put into a true word. It is true enough that the Divinity knows all. But He requires that the true word be said. The mother may know that to maintain life the child requires food. But milk is given when the child asks for it.

H: It is not clear when one should ask God and when one should not. For example, there is a headache that doctors seem unable to cure. I do not ask Swami to cure the headache; I do not pray for a cure. However, in a letter, Swami wrote: 'How is your health? Do not worry about that. Your God is always with you, in you, around you.'

Sai: That is right. What Baba said is enough. For you, body identification is weakening. You have a headache today, a stomach pain tomorrow. Let it go. Don't worry about it. You are not the body. Once Baba has told you not to worry, there is no need to ask Him about it. Don't identify.

H: Does Swami mean that for those persons still fully identified with the body, a continuous headache might be a proper subject for prayer?

Sai: Yes, but why bother Swami about a mere headache? You may tell others the same.

H: Then, it is really all right to ask God?

Sai: When there is a real need, God should be asked to provide. A child asks parents for peppermint candy, and the parents give it. When older, it asks the parents for property, and receives it. It is by right that the child asks, and it is by right that it receives. A child may ask a stranger for peppermint once or twice and expect to receive it. But even if he asks for it, he may not expect to receive property from a stranger. God is not bothered by a multitude of small requests, and He will certainly give property (things of great value). Therefore, one should always ask God to meet needs. It is the individual's right to ask. There is no question of begging.

H: Swami said that in praying to God, the petitioner raises himself to the level of God. In order to make such a prayer, in what state or condition should one first put himself?

Sai: It is not necessary to put oneself into any particular state of meditation.

H: Usually, the idea is that one should go to a quiet place and be in a quiet mood when he wishes to pray.

Sai: Whenever and wherever you put yourself in touch with God, that is the state of meditation. You may feel that 1 p.m. in California is not a good time to call Me, for I may be asleep in India and I should not be disturbed. I know you have felt like that once or twice. But, I am omnipresent; I have no such limitations. I never sleep. In the middle of the night, I turn off the light and rest in bed, because if the light is on, devotees will gather. I have no need of sleep. But you need at least 4 hours of sleep.

H: If I am walking in the street with people around and my mind is engaged with things I must do, is that a good time for prayer?

Sai: At the beginning, one might need some special set of circumstances for clearing the mind for concentration on God. But after a while, if one finds that God is omnipresent and becomes aware of Him and one's thoughts are centered on God, then no matter where you are it is the same. Prayers may be addressed to God and the prayer will reach Him.

H: Swami says that God is omnipresent. What meaning does Swami give the word, 'omnipresent'?

Sai: Omnipresent means everywhere at the same time all the time.

H: If a person does not have any material or worldly needs, then what is the proper subject for prayer?

Sai: Peace of mind. One should pray to God for peace of mind.

H: I am surprised. I thought Swami said that peace of mind has to be secured by oneself working on desires and getting rid of them. And now Swami says we can pray to Him for peace of mind!

Sai: How can you be free of desires? Now, at this moment you are with Swami, and you are free of desires. As soon as your wife has a pain, you have the desire that she will be well, and you pray to Swami to cure her. At any time a desire may come up and where is your peace of mind? Whereas, if God answers your prayer for peace of mind, He must, by having granted that boon, automatically fulfill your needs and desires. First you want a chain from Baba, next day you want something else, a ring; both are made of gold. Why not ask for the gold and then all the desired objects are from that gold.

H: When Swami says, 'peace of mind,' what is the meaning He gives to that phrase?

Sai: There is some small confusion in terms, for there is no mind as such. The mind is a web of desires. Peace of mind is no desires, and in that state there is no mind. Mind is destroyed, so to speak. Peace of mind really means purity, complete purity of consciousness. All spiritual practices are aimed at purification of the heart.

H: Swami, please excuse this question, but it is in everyone's mind. Will Swami come to America soon?

Sai: Baba will delay until a further base is built in America. However, I can go informally anytime. The devotee need only call Me and I will appear at once. Swami has His work to renew India. This must be finished before He is willing to do the same in a foreign country. People generally go to a foreign country with a desire of some sort. Baba has no desire. Of course, foreign individuals come to Baba.

XV

H: What is the most subtle point of Swami's teaching, and then in the circle around that point, what are the things to do in order to realize that most subtle aspect of His teaching?

Sai: The most subtle aspect of Swami's teaching is love. The circle around that subtle point, in order to realize it, is the spiritual practices such as meditation, repetition of the name of the Lord, talking with good people, directing the mind away from harmful thoughts and so on. In themselves, these spiritual practices are of no value. The only thing of real value is love itself. In dealing with people, Swami looks to the good and ignores the bad so as to intensify the good. Swami's teaching, in a way, is like one going into a store to buy sugar. Then one looks at the sugar and buys the sugar and does not bother to become acquainted with all the other details present in the circumstances of the store: the history and character of the storekeeper, his personal relationship with other people, his personal looks, whether he is tall or short or old or young, and so on. The central part of Swami's teaching in regards to living in the world is to see in other people that essential quality which is God and to love that quality and not be bothered by all the other actions, qualities, misbehavior, characteristics of the person. The love of God in the person with whom one is dealing is spiritual love and not physical love. That does not mean in terms of the worldly nature of the being in whom one sees the Lord, and it does not mean that one condones or admires, or does not scold the misbehavior of the worldly part of that person. Even though one sees and loves and really pays attention to God in that person; nevertheless, that person, should be scolded, his attention called to his failures and misbehavings, and so on. And such is not really cruelty. The

45

factor there is the intention; just as in a street fight amongst laborers, one man might scratch the hand of another man with a penknife and cause no wound at all, and yet the police would come and take that man to jail. Whereas in a nearby hospital, a surgeon might take a sharp knife and cut a five-inch gap into a man's body in order to remove an appendix, and that action would be highly rewarded. So in one case the doctor is severely wounding a person and getting praise; and in the other case, a laborer merely scratching a person gets a jail sentence. The whole thing is the intention of the person. Swami sometimes finds it advisable to operate on a person, that is to wound that person, to say something to that person that may hurt him, or to reveal the bad points of that person instead of just looking at the good points. But when Swami does that, the intention behind it is to help the person, and not hurt or harm the patient.

Swami then turned to Hislop and speaking directly to him, said: It is perfectly all right to ask all these questions and clear all your doubts—you are examining Swami and Swami is giving the answers. But when this is all finished, the next time around, Swami will be the examiner and you will be examined and you will have to have the right answers in mind and in heart. Now, all doubts should be emptied so that tomorrow Swami can fill your being with something new, a new oil to bathe the skin, so to speak.

H: One finds himself so faulty there seems to be no possibility of being of any help to others.

Sai: People often think they have to be perfect themselves before they can help anyone else, but such is not the case. If one has a fault or certain weakness, one can point out to others the same weakness that is in oneself. And if those people reply, 'Before you tell me how to behave, why don't you behave?' then one could say that he knows the pain of misbehaving in this fashion and he hopes that the other could avoid the same

46

trouble that oneself was experiencing. In that way it would help to overcome the difficulty in oneself, and while that was being overcome ten more people would be helped. For example, suppose a man had walked along a road covered with thorns that had pierced and torn his feet with great pain and suffering to himself. At the other side of the thorns he sits down to rest, and then sees other people approaching the thorny area. Now, should he beckon them on to come across the thorns and endure the same suffering that he has endured? Surely, that would not be a good deed. Or, should he call to them and warn them that the thorns are there and they should try to find some other way of getting across and reaching their destination? If a person has the humility to recognize the fault in himself and admit that fault, then others will be helped thereby and oneself will be helped. To pretend that one is perfect, to tell people how to behave, pretending that oneself behaves in that perfect fashion, is a great sin, not because it harms the other people, but because it seriously harms oneself.

XVI

Sai: There is One, not two. If one sees a second, then Maya is in operation.

H: Life appears to be somewhat a jungle of unexpected dangers!

Sai: Maya is harmless to the devotee of God. That same Maya, so dangerous to the person who does not believe in God, protects the devotee from all harm. The cat carries the kitten in the mouth from here to there, and the kitten is unharmed. But a rat is killed by a cat. It is the same mouth in both cases. Maya brings trouble, yet it is the same Maya that tenderly protects the devotee of God.

H: Then, the devotee of God may just do his work and not worry about penetrating the illusions of Maya?

Sai: Yes. The devotee may do work for God and pay no

attention to the powers of Maya. God protects His devotees. His devotee is near and dear to God, and He carries the devotee safely through life. In Indian kitchens there is an instrument— tongs—that is used to pick up and move the cooking utensil. The instrument can seize everything except the user. Maya is the tongs held and used by God.

H: Then God holds Maya in one hand and the devotee in the other?

Sai: Two hands are not needed; one hand is enough. If God held the devotee with one hand, the tongs might still seize him! So God holds both in the same hand.

XVII

H: What does Swami say about the three states of consciousness?

Sai: There is waking, sleeping and dreaming, and deep sleep. In deep sleep there is no mind. All are changing states. The past is gone, the future is coming, the present is leaving. None of these changing states is truth; for all agree that truth is real and the same whether in past, present or future. You are always that truth; changeless, constant, unaffected by change, always the same.

H: Swami says that 'I' refers to the body. But when one thinks of himself he sees not just the body, but also his mind, his conditioning, and his tendencies.

Sai: 'Body' means all the five senses and all that is implied by any extension of these.

H: In deep sleep, the body is gone and the mind is gone. But there is a strong happiness. However, that happiness is only known afterwards as memory, and memory is just a thought. It has no reality.

Sai: The difference between deep sleep and samadhi is that in samadhi the happiness is known at the time it occurs.

H: Swami says that in samadhi, happiness is known at the

time that it occurs. But how could the person, the subject, be aware of himself as happy? Surely that implies a subject-object relationship. Subject-object is unreal, so experience in those terms must also be unreal, mustn't it?

Sai: If one looks in the mirror and sees dust on the brow, he will at once remove it, even though he was unaware of it before looking in the mirror. The guru is the mirror.

XVIII

H: Once he has tasted sugar, one never mistakes salt for sugar. If that bliss of which Swami speaks is our real nature, how is it that we confuse the unreal for the real?

Sai: You have not tasted either the salt or the sugar, but are just looking at them and imagining them.

H: When one is merged in the Divine bliss, is one aware of it?

Sai: He is the witness of his bliss. The person loses his limited awareness for God's total awareness. Deep sleep is samadhi, where there is no world and no mind but only the experience of 'I.' Freedom is that same experience in full awareness.

H: At various times, Swami mentions happiness, joy, bliss. Is there a difference?

Sai: Happiness is temporary; it is given to us by others. Next comes joy. One is joyful while filling the stomach—it comes and goes. But bliss is one's rightful nature; it does not come and go. Bliss is not something that comes to one; it is one's real nature and is permanent.

H: If one is wholly absorbed in God, who will take care of the body?

Sai: In waking and dreams, the mind is there, but who takes care in deep sleep? God takes care. Who takes care of the body at any time? One side may be paralyzed; can you make it move? The genuine saints and yogis in the Himalayas—they have no way to take care of their bodies. It is God who takes care.

H: Baba says that in sadhana, at a certain stage the exterior nature ceases. How is that?

Sai: There are ten stages in sadhana, each cognized by sounds of various types ranging from just sound, through vibrations, bell, flute, conch, Om, thunder, explosion. The 10th is pure form. Then the senses are transcended. Until then, everything is in the sense realm. Above the senses, there is the state of bliss, the universal body of God, which is light.

H: Is that state of bliss there only for a time? What happens then in the daily round of living?

Sai: That state, when fully realized as natural, always remains. Then the world is bliss, always bliss. Think God, eat God, drink God, breathe God, live God.

H: Does everyone pass through these sadhana stages?

Sai: No. One may go directly to the transcendental state, or to the stage number 6 or 7 or any way at all. It is not uniform.

H: What should be one's attitude to these sadhana stages as one encounters them?

Sai: The states change, but the attitude should be unchanging.

H: But what value should one give to the various stages?

Sai: The sadhaka will not be satisfied with any of the states because it is complete union that is desired. Desire remains strong and constant until the transcendental bliss is realized and then desire ceases. Who is the poorest man in the world?

H: The man without God?

Sai: No. The man with the most desires is the most poor. Until we realize the desireless state of pure bliss, we are in poverty.

A Visitor: One gains a measure of spiritual understanding, but in the next life it is all swept away and all is lost?

Sai: We say, 'I am not the body, mind or intelligence, because they are impermanent.' These are of the same matter. They are not of different material. Just as butter, curds, buttermilk, ghee cannot again be joined to the others to once again constitute milk, in the same way the quality of spiritual being, once separated by churning the milk of the world, does not go back again into the world. The spiritual beingness is never lost once it is manifested.

XIX

H: This car in which we are driving has certain natural factors that are neither good nor bad. If moving, it has speed and momentum. In like fashion, what are the natural powers of the mind?

Sai: The mind does not have any powers. The only power is Atma Shakthi, the power of the Atma. Actually, the mind does not exist. There is no mind. The moon is lighted by the sun. What we see is the reflected light of the sun. What we take to be the mind is the reflected light of the Atma shining on the heart. Really, there is only the heart. The reflected light is taken to be the mind, but that is just a way of looking at it, a concept. There is just the sun and the moon. (The reflected light is not a third object.) In another way, the mind cannot be compared to a car. A car has form. The mind has no form, for the mind has no existence of its own. The mind can be said to be woven of desires. The Atma shines on the heart, whether the heart be pure or impure. If the heart is purified and if the strongest desire is for God, that is best.

H: My mind and intelligence are in operation at this very moment, regardless of the subtlety or coarseness of quality. Baba says that the only power is the Atma power. So why do I not see as Atma, that which is in operation through the mind-intelligence complex at this very moment?

Sai: The Atma in its purity will be seen when the hindrances to clear vision are removed by spiritual practice, by sadhana. Real sadhana is not just sitting in meditation. Meditation is constant inner enquiry as to who am 'I,' what is loving, and what is harsh. Meditation is thinking about spiritual principles, searching out the application to oneself of what Baba says, and so on.

H: I have a conviction so strong that it is into the marrow of my bones that life is one, and that other beings and myself are one. The Atma is that One, and it is fully here at this moment and I am constantly engaged in sadhana so the question remains, 'Why do I not actually experience that unity as no other than myself?'

Sai: Your conviction of unity is an idea, a thought. It is not experience. For instance, your wife has a chest pain. Do you have the chest pain? If not, where is the unity? The unity of life must be experienced—not an idea or thought without experience.

H: Now! Swami has to say something about experience! If sadhana and conviction do not bring that unity as real experience, then how is one to get it?

Sai: With steady sadhana, no special effort is needed to try and get the experience of One. Just as with ourselves in this car. We need only concern ourselves with the careful driving of the car, and in due course we will arrive at Anantapur. With correct and steady sadhana, in due course, the actual experience of One will naturally come about.

H: Swami, it is not possible to tell death to wait for a convenient time. In respect to death, in what state should the mind be?

Sai: That we feel that only oneself will not die is the greatest wonder. Flowers bloom and give perfume before dropping. Whereas man, when his end is approaching, has only a long face. He should be like the flower and do something good and bright when dying. There are two things to remember: Death and God. And there are two things to forget: any harm done to us by others and any good we may have done to others. For to hold these two would be to reach for future results and there will be future consequences if these are held in the mind. Whatever we think, or put in mind, we experience the reaction. Of course, death should be held in the mind always; for then much good action will result and much harmful action will be avoided.

H: The mind is said to be dangerous. What does that mean?

Sai: It is the same mind that can liberate or enslave. The mind is like a snake with long poison fangs. When the poison is removed from those fangs, then the danger is removed. In like fashion, when desire disappears, the danger of the mind disappears.

H: But it is always said that all troubles arise from the mind?

Sai: From desires!

H: Then, one should control one's thoughts?

Sai: Thoughts and desires are not the same. There are many thoughts that are not desires. If thoughts go too deeply into objects, desires arise. If there is a desire, there was a thought. But not all thoughts are desires. Dark clouds bring rain, but there can be clouds without rain. God's grace is in drops like rain. They accumulate and then there is a torrent. If there is a very strong desire for God, even bad thoughts just pass through the mind and are not held. Desire directed to God brings discrimination. Intelligence, which is discrimination, is not the mind, nor is it thoughts. Intelligence is a direct Atma Shakthi, a direct force of the Atma.

A Visitor: How is one to handle bad thoughts arising from envy, hatred, laziness?

Sai: There is no use resisting or fighting thoughts. If suppressed, they are always ready to spring forth at weak moments—like snakes in a basket. If the cover gets loose or is removed the snakes spring forth. The way to overcome bad thoughts and impulses is by having thoughts of serving the Lord, good conversation with wise people, good actions and words. The weight of good acts and thoughts will bury the seeds of bad actions and thoughts. Both good and bad thoughts and impulses are like seeds in the mind. If buried too deeply in the earth, seeds rot and waste away. Good thoughts and deeds bury

53

bad seeds so deeply that they rot and pass away and are no longer ready to spring forth.

H: Swami, when thoughts are troublesome, I say, '*Thy* mind, Swami; it is not mine,' and that particular thought stream stops.

Sai: That is right. At that moment there is no ego. That is the easy path.

H: Swami, what does the mind know? There is much knowledge in the mind, but what does it really know?

Sai: The mind does not know anything. So-called education is just book knowledge. Hand in hand with knowledge must go philosophy. Philosophy is not religion, it is love for God. It is cultured by reciting the Name, singing bhajans, thinking spiritual thoughts, desiring union with God. Union with God, as the bubble upon breaking, finds itself the whole ocean. From the cultivation of philosophy comes will power. Without will power, knowledge is useless.

H: Swami, in the West, will power is thought of as a quality one is born with.

Sai: Will power is brought about by philosophy. Will power is the direct manifestation of the Atma Shakthi.

H: In the West, great value is given to the mind. It is felt that unless one develops a skilful mind, he cannot gain success in life. For instance, I needed to develop skill of mind to get an education and earn money to travel and see Baba.

Sai: You came to see Baba because of the heart, not the mind, isn't it? The viewpoint that there is a mind is useful up to a certain stage—university, science, and so forth. But after a certain stage, science falls away and philosophy comes to the front. Heart is then used instead of mind. The other day, someone mentioned the illustration of the mirror. As one moves away, the image grows smaller and smaller, although actually, the image has not changed at all. The same happens with the world. As one turns to God with stronger and stronger love, the world recedes, appearing smaller and smaller until it can hardly be noticed at all. Really, there is only the heart.

H: The belief that we are self-willed, separate beings moving about in the world—what is the cause of this illusion?

Sai: The whole mirage, the whole thing, arises from the 'I' thought. From identification with the body, all complications arise. Since it is the mind that has woven this web of identification with the body, it is the mind that must now turn and seek one's true nature through enquiry, discrimination, and renunciation.

H: Swami has said that the mind need not be dangerous. But with all the trouble it has brought about, it seems to be very dangerous.

Sai: The mind creates no harm and gives no trouble as long as it is not merged with the body senses. For instance, the mind has a thought of the theatre. No harm. But if the mind picks up the body and carries it to the theatre, then it becomes involved with the picture, the people, the emotions, the concepts, and peace is lost. The mind should not engage itself in body senses. Body sense should serve the needs of body only. Mind should be engaged in the five mind senses, which are: truth, concentration, peace, love, bliss. As long as the mind is so engaged, all is well and the person is happy and peaceful. Physical objects have a temperature potential. If the breathing is fast movement, body temperature rises. If objects subject to temperature are added to a fire, the fire burns more fiercely. That which is subject to temperature may join with that which is subject to temperature. Mind, however, has no temperature. God is without temperature. So mind and God may merge.

H: In this, Swami, what is the definition of 'mind'?

Sai: The whole complex, ego through intelligence may justly be called 'mind.'

H: Whenever the mind falls away from necessary work, I call it to attention and keep it engaged in repeating, 'Sai Ram, Sai Ram.' Is that all right?

Sai: Quite all right.

H: When the mind is not engaged in any particular work, where should the attention be kept?

Sai: Between the eyebrows. That is the Eye of Wisdom, of Siva.

H: The flow of thought interferes with concentration. How can one diminish thinking?

Sai: The habit of thinking is long standing. Even if the habit is broken, there is a slow cessation. For example, a fan continues to revolve for a time after the switch is turned off. But the train of thought can be changed. One train of thought can stop another. The best way is to divert the train of thought to a spiritual topic. The attraction to God is spontaneous. It is the turning back to the source; all other attractions are self-imposed. The fish is placed in a gold and jewel vase of greatest value, but it has no interest in the gold and jewels, it wants only to get back to the sea. Man comes into his limitation from his home. He is really of the nature of God, of this Ocean of Delight, of Rama, of He who attracts. The Soul attracts us. Rama was God, that Ocean of Delight in human form. Everybody wanted to be close to Him, to look at Him.

H: Well, Swami, perhaps if one were to follow thought inward to its source and observe the source of thought, one might then have a quiet mind? In affairs of the world thought is both necessary and practical. But when there is no need to be thinking, the mind still keeps on going with all sorts of idle thoughts; whereas one would be much better off if the mind would just be quiet.

Sai: That is really the wrong way to approach the matter. The nature of the mind is restless, just like a rat whose nature is always to nibble at something, and just like a snake whose nature is to be biting at something. The nature of the mind is to be occupied. Even when still, like the feathers on a peacock, there is a shimmering, an apparent movement in the mind. Like the aspen tree, even on a still morning its leaves seem to tremble and move. It is the nature of the mind to dwell upon things. So, the proper method to deal with the mind is to direct the mind's activity towards good deeds, good thoughts, repetition of the name of the Lord, and not allow it to be aimed at harmful objects, harmful thoughts and deeds. In that way, the mind's natural tendency to be occupied will be fulfilled and yet it will keep out of mischief. Another essential to keeping the mind away from harmful activities is work. Man is made to work hard, and if one is working hard in service to the Lord in one way or the other, the mind will not have time to be occupied with useless, random thoughts. And if there is no outside work, then the work of spiritual endeavor should go on, in the way of meditation, recitation of the Name, reading good books, talking with good people, and so on. One might find it difficult to surrender to God, but every man surrenders to time, and time is God. Day by day one's life is shortened and one surrenders his life to that time; time conquers one's life and that time is God. Therefore, first there is work, then wisdom, then love, and the time will come in a person's life when work itself is love, or work itself is God.

H: But Swami said the other day that if the mind were quiet and receptive, then perhaps Swami would come into the mind and speak.

Sai: If the desire to communicate with Swami is sufficiently intense and strong, then the mind will be sufficiently quiet for Swami to speak; but the problem is that we do not have that intensity in our lives.

H: The Buddha's way of slowing down the mind is given much attention in Burma. Swami must have a better way?

Sai: The Buddha's way of watching the breath as it enters and leaves the nostrils is just a beginning; just for a few minutes before the meditation begins. There is no 'better' way to quiet the mind. There is only one way. Sitting in meditation, the question often comes up, 'How long should we sit.' There is no answer. There is no particular time. Meditation is really an all-day-long process. The sun shines, and the sunlight falls here and there. What is the difference between the sun and the sunlight?

H: There is no difference, Swami.

Sai: In the same way, all is God. Thoughts, desires, all are God. All thoughts should be regarded as God.

H: But Swami, there is still the puzzle of how to slow down the activity of the mind.

Sai: Really, there is no mind; it is a question of what is desired. With God as the only desire, all will be well.

H: But in meditation there is a fast rush of thoughts and ideas through the mind. Does this not need to be slowed down so there may be quiet in meditation?

Sai: Yes. The mind must slow down. At a certain stage it will come to a stop. If desire in meditation is turned towards union with God, the mind will naturally slow down. No method should be used; no force used. Desire should not be too fast, too strong. Even desire for God can be too hurried, too feverish. Start early, drive slowly, reach safely. It is possible to be too lazy. Fast, then slow is also bad. The process should be steady.

H: These thoughts that stream through the mind, are they material?

Sai: Yes. They are matter. All matter is impermanent.

H: Where do thoughts come from?

Sai: They come from food and environment. If you have sathwic food and have only desire for good, only good thoughts will come.

H: Where do thoughts go?

Sai: They go no place because thoughts do not flow through the mind. The mind goes out and grasps and gets engaged in thoughts. If desire is for God, the mind does not go out. But the best way is to not have the problem of getting rid of thoughts. The best way is to see all thoughts as God. Then only God thoughts will come.

H: Swami says that it is the Atma that is unlimited power, yet in one's daily life, the mind gives the experience of being a sort of relentless power.

Sai: The mind is passive, yet it seems to be active. It is active only because the Atma reflects into it. It sometimes seems to be stronger than Atma. Iron, in its nature, is not hot; it

58

is cool and passive. The iron is heated in fire. Is it the iron that burns, thus creating the heat? No, it is the heat that is put into the iron by the burning coals. The heat is added to the iron. Yet, when hot, the iron seems even more hot than the burning coals.

H: The mind has the tendency to plan ahead. No doubt this is a wrong activity?

Sai: In ordinary life, one makes plans and carries them out. This has to continue, with purity, and without harm to others. At length, a spontaneous divine thought will arise without planning. Such divine impulses will continue.

A Visitor: How can I tell what is right thought?

Sai: Here, in the Ashram, you can ask Swami. In America, pray for the answer, then make enquiry in an impersonal way, and in half an hour you will have the answer. If you know what is right, don't ask. Do it. That is confidence, God power. Put aside all relationships. Is the work right, regardless of who is involved?

H: Swami says to keep a distance from the mind. What does that mean?

Sai: That means, do not be led by the mind.

H: What are the acceptable mental functions?

Sai: First, find out what is right and what is wrong. If right, do that which satisfies you. If unsure, do nothing until sure.

XX

H: Swami mentions Vedanta. What is the correct use of that word?

Sai: Vedanta is metaphysical enquiry of the divine, the world, and the valid experience of each. Metaphysics begins where physics ends. Vedanta proves by experience that which has been formulated. Philosophy is the fruit which has all the parts, whereas Vedanta is the sweet juice. Philosophy takes you to the edge of truth, gives you a vision of truth. Vedanta takes you into the heart of truth. Philosophy is a way of intellectual enquiry.

H: Swami speaks of the divine, the world and the individual. What is the relationship of Swami to the individual?

Sai: Swami is the activator of the individual. He is the 'I,' the Self in you and in everyone else. Sun is reflected in the water, and the water becomes warm. Yet, warmth is not in water's nature.

H: What is the difference between God and the world?

Sai: Only in words, in the mind, is there a difference. When one is fully devoted to God, desiring Him only, the verbal and conceptual differentiation will cease, and the world also will be seen as God. The sequence should be experienced and seen as God, life, world. But most people see the world, life—and God is far distant.

A Visitor: Why is creation? What is the reason for it?

Sai: First ask, 'Why food?' No reason. 'Why marriage?' No reason. Then children. 'Why children?' No reason. It is your wish. Creation is God's wish, His sankalpa. There is a seed of a tree. It sprouts and there are many twigs and branches—and more and more. Thousands of leaves grow, and hundreds of fruits. There is diversity. All from a single seed.

Visitor: But what is behind creation? What is the reason?

Sai: First ask, 'Who are you?'

Visitor: I am a nobody.

Sai: No. No. Who are you? First find that and then you will find the answer to your question.

Visitor: Is there life on other planets?

Sai: Creation is endless.

H: Is it that man creates his world by projecting concepts? For example: 'table' is not real. It is the wood that forms the table that is real, yet we accept the concept 'table' as being real, and we act according to that concept.

Sai: The table is wood, and 'table' is a projection of the human mind, and 'table' is only temporary. But the image in the mind is in the nature of an archetype. Likewise, castles in clouds are passing phenomena, but God is their base; just as waves, spray, bubbles arising from the ocean fall away and disappear, but the ocean does not disappear.

H: Swami once said that the world emerges outward from man, just as human beings emerge outward from the body of the mother. Does this mean the entire world of which we are aware, everything?

Sai: There is one exception. There is one thing that comes into man from the outside. That thing is the ego, which is formed by attachment to outside objects. With desire for the world cut, ego automatically vanishes. Impressions that are taken into man from outside, if taken as reality, are harmful. Because man looks at something outside and then creates, he thinks he is reproducing the outside. Whereas, in fact, the outside thing seen merely recalls to memory that which is already within. When the eyes are open, one sees creation. All beings are created by the help of the eyes. The source of all that you see is the eyes. All so seen is impermanent. The three letters in 'eye' represent the three gunas. But with 'I,' the Self, one can see something quite beyond the transient.

H: Would Swami please explain his statement that the world is a mirror?

Sai: The world is a mirror and life is the reflection of God. If the mirror is pure, only God is seen. The opposites, good and bad, are no longer seen at all. There is only God. If the world is not seen, then there is neither mirror nor any reflection. We have the idea of the world only because of the mirror effect. The mirror (world) exists only as long as our desires exist. 'World' means the inside sense world. We apprehend the world through the senses. These senses are seen outside. It is only because of the illusion of the senses that there appears to be a body. A corpse is burned when the wood is set afire. The inner senses correspond to the wood. When they are burned through enquiry and sadhana, the body automatically disappears. Both enquiry and practice are necessary.

H: But, Swami, our experience is that objects exist independent of our consciousness of them.

Sai: For us the world exists only if we are there to see it. If we are blind, we do not see it. If we are in a faint, it does not exist for us. For us, the world is as we see it. It takes shape for us according to our viewpoint. If our viewpoint is that all is God, then everything we see is God. Suppose we take a picture with a camera. Do the trees enter the lens and impress themselves on the film, or does the camera reach out and grasp the trees?

H: The trees impress themselves on the camera.

Sai: Wrong! I take a picture of a person who does not want his picture taken. Will the refusal prevent the picture? Or, put it the other way. The person wants his picture taken. Will that result in the picture? The heart is like a film that can capture the image of Swami. If the film is latent and clean, it can capture Swami even if he does not want. But if the camera is without such a film, if the heart is impure and clouded, then Swami's image cannot be there even if he wants. The body is the camera, the mind is the lens, the intelligence is the switch, and love is the film.

H: But Swami's image in the heart is His form. Krishna says, 'The devotee need picture the Paramatma as unpicturable, that is enough.' What does that mean, and how does it apply to the image of Swami in the heart?

Sai: The image need not be that of Swami. It may be love, which is Swami. First, God is realized in form. Then He is seen everywhere in that form. Then God may be realized without form, since all form is impermanent. A child, learning, sees an elephant statue. On the statue, 'elephant' is written in words. The child cannot read the words, but he learns about 'elephant' from its name as he hears it. Once he has learned to read, then just the word remains and from that he understands 'elephant.' The statue, the form, is impermanent, but the word remains as long as the language endures. The word 'elephant' represents elephant in its formless state. Likewise, once the devotee learns the language of divinity, then God need not be pictured; the word is enough. But one learns about God through form and name.

H: We see here the form of God, as Swami. How are we to understand that form? Does God appear only as that one form? If the question is improper, may Swami please disregard it.

Sai: The question is all right. Wires in the room are everywhere, but only one bulb is connected into the wires. Only the one light is seen in full power. The same current is in all the wires. The Avatar is one only, and this one body is taken by the Avatar. Of course, a brilliant light spreads outward into rays, but the rays are not different from the light.

H: Swami, please go a little deeper into 'form' and 'formless.'

Sai: The body is not the truth we attribute to it. An example: For 30 years a man worships the mother who gave him birth. He massages her feet, prostrates before her, gazes into her eyes with love, listens to her voice, is warmed and made happy by her affectionate and loving regard. At age 60, the mother dies. At once the son cries out, 'Mother, Mother, why have you left me? To whom did the man cry out? The body he worshipped was there, the feet he massaged daily were there, but he cried out that his mother was not there, that she had left him. We have to conclude that even though the man had for the past 30 years regarded the body and mother as one and the same, yet when mother died he instantly knew that mother was not body and that mother had departed even though body remained. So, of what value was the body which never was mother even though for a time it had been regarded as mother? Contemplating this mystery, it is apparent that had it not been for the body, mother could not have been known. It was only through the medium of the body that the man had been able to experience and thus know the tender, loving, sublime quality of mother which resulted in love rising up in his heart. The formless, timeless quality of 'mother' could be known and attained only through the impermanent form.

H: Swami! This is wonderful! This explains the real significance of form!

Sai: The same is true of the formless, transcendent divine. Without form, it is non-existent for us. We become cognizant of the divine through the medium of form.

H: Sai has told us the secret of form and formless! How is transition made from worship of God in form to worship of the formless divine?

Sai: Transition is made by full adoration of God in form, then seeing that beloved form in everyone, then God is everyplace and loving others comes naturally and easily.

H: When Swami is present, His form is easily seen and may be worshipped, but when Swami's physical person is absent, should one form a mental image of Him so that one may continue to see His form?

Sai: Yes. One should have a mental image of a form of God, fully developed, the mind poured into that form. When the image of God is seen outside, it is qualified dualism. When seen in the mind it is qualified monism. When the form is absorbed into the Atma, that is Advaita, non-dualism. The two preliminary steps are not separate stages; they are contained in Advaita, as buttermilk and butter are contained in milk. The image of God seen outside should be taken into the mind and then into the soul.

H: What is the best way to form the mental image of God?

Sai: If you wish, the form you see can be taken as an image. Or a photograph can be taken.

H: If a photo of Swami, or the directly perceived image of Swami is taken as the mental image, no doubt the concentration should not waver from the chosen image?

Sai: The mind should be steady on the one chosen image of God. When an image is made of silver, the eyes, hair, mouth, skin—all are silver.

H: Please say that again?

Sai: The mind is poured into the mold of the image so that the mind is the image of God.

H: I see. That is most enlightening! But Swami, we feel happier when in Swami's physical presence and not so happy when Swami is away.

Sai: You are identified with your physical form and so you look to the form of another. When you are less attached to physical form, your happiness will be even more.

XXI

H: One regards himself as a son of Swami. Swami is as the Mother, and we confide in Him, directly if possible, but if not, then by prayer and by writing to him.

Sai: There is an endless flow of letters coming to Swami. Swami reads all the letters and, about 10 a.m., the letters are burned. Swami does everything himself, so everything is done right. Swami never sleeps. In the middle of the night, he turns off the light and rests in bed because if the light is on devotees gather. Swami has no need of sleep. But men need at least four hours of sleep; it is essential for them. People think that Baba rests in the afternoon until 4 p.m. But he never rests. He is never tired. He is always working. People are upset when three or four relatives visit. But Baba's visitors are endless. Baba is attending to every detail of his schools and colleges, and to the millions of his devotees. And, for most people, the responsibility for their work rests elsewhere, but Baba is responsible for the results as well as for the work.

H: Baba is responsible also for His other worlds, is He not?

Sai: Yes. For saints, rishis, yogis everywhere, Swami is attending to the guidance, protection and welfare of these wherever they may be.

H: I mean, Swami is responsible for the entire universe, not just this world?

Sai: It is like this. Baba is the switch. The switch is turned on and all goes forward automatically. As the key is turned in a car, then all parts of the car work automatically. In a similar way, the universe is automatically regulated. So-called 'miracles' are not miracles, nor do they prove divinity. Baba's endless work in all the worlds is easy, no weight, always happy—that is the 'miracle.'

H: Considering the endless problems that Swami deals with in this world, it is strange that He is always in bliss, always happy.

Sai: Regardless of events, Swami is always happy, always blissful.

H: Please excuse a question that may seem rude: Swami seems to have different moods. What does this mean?

Sai: A boat glides over the flood but does not allow the flood to enter it. Just as one is at peace in a boat into which no water comes, no worries or concerns enter into Baba's state of bliss. But ordinary men do not do the same as Baba. They allow 'water,' all sorts of worries and concerns to enter the 'boat,' and there is no happiness, no bliss, no peace of mind. Baba's bliss is ever present, regardless of the world. Consider, Baba each month must meet an expense budget of hundreds of thousands of rupees. On his shoulders rest all the affairs of the schools, the ashram, the people within his physical circle, the interviews, the petitions, the correspondence, the problems. That is on the body level. At the same time, on the mental level, Baba is with those who yearn for God, no matter in what area of the world, saints, yogis, rishis, spiritual aspirants everywhere, watching them, guiding them, fostering every movement of heart or mind towards God. But Baba is untouched by all this. His bliss is constant, unchanging. Even outwardly his bliss is constant, even though it may appear that he is angry, impatient, aloof, distant. The 'anger' is just sound, because the sound of anger is necessary to correct certain situations. In like fashion, 'aloofness' or 'distance' is just the appropriate role at that time and place. In fact, Baba's love is constant and unchanging, just as is His bliss.

H: Baba has the inconceivably immense task of the universe. How can He afford to spend time talking to people like us?

Sai: Baba, with his limitless bodies, is everywhere doing the tasks, 'a thousand heads, hands, feet—Sahasra sheersha purushah sahasraksha sahasrapad—.' It is just this body that sits here talking with you. That is Baba's omnipresence. The Avatar is beyond the 5 elements. He is the Creator. Arjuna was the controller, Krishna the Creator. Science is outside; wisdom is inside. Man, turning outward, creates machines, but there his control ends. Witness the three dead astronauts of a few months ago. God is not subject to any limitation. He is the Creator of the elements, their Modifier, their Preserver, their Destroyer.

H: The Avatar is never born, but He appears to take birth in a body which then gradually grows to full size in the ordinary way. The bodies that one sees are impermanent, and Baba does not look to be different.

Sai: The Avatar takes only the one body such as you have described. The difference is that men come into bodies with tendencies and the results of actions. Baba takes this body without any tendencies, completely free, no desires, no attachments, always happy.

H: When one sees Baba as a form amongst all the perishable forms, cannot one point to Him as the one reality amongst all these perishable dream-like forms?

Sai: Yes. The one reality is Baba. 'Baba' means, Being, Awareness, Bliss, Atma, one Reality.

XXII

H: What did Baba mean about the spiritual rays that comprise a human being being projected into the vastness, instead of the limited ego?

Sai: When the world melts away, when there is bliss, or even when there is a temporary feeling of happiness, hold to that state and stay with it, and do not allow yourself to fall back into ego emotions and thoughts. From man comes a series of spiritual rays whose quality is delight, bliss. All man need do is to manifest that bliss. The idea of search is in error. Everyone

67

already knows the truth. All that is needed is to put that truth into practice, to manifest it. The humanity of man is just these spiritual rays of delight. It is very easy to crush a flower, or to wink an eye. Self-realization is as easy as that.

H: Swami said that it is man's duty to be happy.

Sai: Happiness is essential for God-realization. It is one of the major gates to divinity. It is not just a fault if a person is not happy; it is one of the most serious of all faults. It is a barrier to Realization. Mostly, people are unhappy because of worldly pursuits, attachments, enjoyments. Too much interested in the world. To get free of this fault, a person has to be told of the seriousness of the fault. He should realize that desire is never-ending, like the waves of the sea.

H: Swami says that pleasure or happiness is the interval between two sorrows. What is the implication?

Sai: Pleasure is an interval between two sorrows. Remove the sorrow and only pleasure, delight remains. But nobody troubles to find the cause of sorrow. It is like the lady who went to look for a lost needle under the street lamp because there was no light in the house where she had lost the article. The house is lighted by the light of wisdom. The lost item must be found where it was lost. Actually, sorrow, or pain is caused by desire. The cure is to use that same desire and turn it to God, to desire God. Instantly, suffering will cease because the cause, turning from God to worldly desire, has been eliminated. The incidents that caused sorrow will cease to cause sorrow. If a person called 'my' suffers, there is a direct pain in oneself. But if one's desire is for God only, that pain will cease.

H: But one suffers also because of the pain he is aware of in another.

Sai: The suffering one feels for other people who one sees suffering, is from imagination. That sympathetic suffering will leave, but the sympathy remains. Compassion is when love is mobile and flows. Personal love is when love is not mobile but remains fixed on husband, wife, child, etc. Devotion is that free mobile flow of love to God.

68

XXIII

H: Last night, in speaking to the students, Swami said something very puzzling; that another person's sins would pass to oneself through the touch of that person's skin.

Sai: It is for that reason that devotees are not allowed to touch the feet of some swamis. Since one cannot be sure who is bad and who is good, it is best to refrain from touching.

A Visitor: Is that why Indians greet people by that kind of salute, instead of by much handshaking as is done in the West?

Sai: No. That is not the reason.

H: Does Swami mean that if I touch a person, I then commit sin in the same way as he?

Sai: When the tender plant of devotion begins to grow, it must be protected. When a young tree is growing, various animals will eat it and may kill it. For this reason a fence is placed around the young tree to protect it. When the tree is grown it needs no protection. The same animals who would have first destroyed it, now seek and find shade and shelter beneath its branches. When devotion has grown strong and intense, it will burn all sins. Until then, the person whose devotion is just new, must see bad as bad, and good as good. The person grown strong in his devotion may see bad as good, and see good only. It is not just physical touch wherein lies the danger, but in mental intimacy also; bad influences may flow from one person to the other. Your children are not your children, they are God's children. You should love them, but your thoughts should not pass to them. There is body relationship with mother, from whose body you came, and with grandmother from whose body mother came. Sisters and brothers are to be treated with respect. But with other people, there is no body relationship.

XXIV

H: I gave Swami a ring created by a yogi. I did not want to wear it and I didn't know what to do with it. That is, I sent it up to Swami by a messenger with a note about it.

Sai: That was another attempt aimed at you by other interests. You are known as a devotee of Baba, and it was an attempt to interest you elsewhere. Like that western city matter. You should reject such attempts out-of-hand.

H: But that man from there said Swami stayed at his house.

Sai: Not true. That area is strongly Communist. At one time Baba did bring about genuine evidence of his sankalpa there, but ego and money-making arose, so Baba stopped things. Again he allowed it, and now he has again stopped it. Those people, in fear of loss of reputation, are now doing things by tricks.

H: The man seemed a very nice fellow.

Sai: Not so. There is always good and bad in dualistic phenomena. When there is an Avatar, there must always be the bad. Rama's foster-mother was his enemy. Krishna's uncle was his enemy even before he was born. Shirdi Baba was much abused. Not long ago, there was a man who challenged Swami to some tests. Stories appeared over a broad area, even in other countries. This man had some foreign people in his camp. Some of Swami's devotees urged him to reply. But reply would have been shameful. This yogi was eating nails and glass and so on. He created a special tank for a test of water walking. Why a special tank? Something crooked. He sold tickets to spectators for up to 100 rupees and more per ticket. On the appointed day he stepped on the water and sank. The police had to put him in a cell to protect him from abuse and all the money was refunded. Now, people said, what a fool he had been to challenge Swami. His disaster was a result of the foolish challenge. Later, the man wrote to Swami disclaiming any serious intent to challenge and confessed that he had used Swami's name just to

70

increase ticket sales. The man is gone and now nothing is heard from him.

H: But Swami, why would the man be so foolish as to try to walk on water without practicing beforehand?

Sai: The man was walking on water. But ego and greed arose, and that finished it. Thought, word, and deed must be the same.

XXV

In the car enroute to Anantapur, an American who was teaching at the Sathya Sai College at Brindavan said: Swami, I feel guilty about leaving my classes.

Sai: Duty in the world carries no force or weight when God calls. God is the goal of life. When in His company, there is no duty. When He is absent on tour, etc., then duty comes into full play, because duty is God.

H: When I am absent from Swami's physical person and far away in America, I know of His actual Presence by the jasmine perfume. Someone said it was smelled by the smell sense of the subtle body, is this correct?

Sai: No. Senses are in the physical body. The subtle body does not have senses. The perfume is known by the physical senses.

H: Does man have three bodies?

Sai: Yes. There is Body, Mind, and Soul; physical body, subtle body, and causal body. On death, the physical and subtle bodies disintegrate, but the causal body remains.

H: How about the five kosas, the five sheaths?

Sai: The food sheath, life sheath and mind sheath are impermanent. The intelligence sheath and bliss sheath remain. The body is mud. Out of the mud everything grows. Only the body dies. Life and all the senses merge into mind. Mind merges into wisdom. Wisdom merges into bliss, into God. Thus are the five sheaths.

H: What are the 14 lokas, the 14 worlds?

Sai: They are really thoughts. There are seven levels of thought ascending upward, and seven downward.

H: Swami, some people claim to travel on the astral plane by projecting their minds.

Sai: It is like dreams or visions; it is not real. However, if a vision appears in meditation, it is of something real.

H: Time is set by the clock, and on the clock each minute is the same as the next. But in one's life, time goes slowly in one experience and extremely fast in the next.

Sai: Hislop goes to sleep in Bombay. He dreams that he is born in California, and he lives through 65 years of life. Yet this entire 65 years takes only two minutes of clock time. Hislop has gone to sleep in Bombay, but the Bombay body is left behind. This is proof that Hislop is not that body. To the jnani, who has wakened to wisdom, 65 years of 'waking life' is just a moment— like the dream to Hislop.

H: What is this present moment?

Sai: God is omnipresent. That is, He is ever present. This moment is God. There is only God. Truth is the same in the past, in the present, and it will remain the same in the future. Therefore, the time sequence of past, present, future is just imagination. But 'I' am timeless, beyond time. 'I' look at past, present, future; they are not me. Of course, past, present, and future must be taken into account in daily affairs. These two aspects of time must be mixed and in operation at the same time. The perception that the time sequence is only imagination, that 'I' am timeless and beyond time; both should be there at the very moment that one is using the time sequence in his daily affairs.

H: In terms of the unreality of time, how are we to experience past, present, future?

Sai: They are unreal. But at the same time the Atma is real. Hold to that central reality. There need be no confusion. The inward intelligence may harmonize the experience of the relative time and the permanent Self. Even now you are hearing and seeing, yet the inward intelligence co-ordinates the two.

H: At this moment we seem to be as we are at this moment. When Swami looks at us with His eyes, what is it that He sees?

Sai: Man has two eyes; he sees only past and present. God has three eyes. God's eyes are spiritual. He sees in front, behind, above, below. Like the garland pulled over the finger—finger is the present and it is in touch with past and future. God is the present. He is omnipresent. As Baba looks at people, he sees the past, the present moment, the future and everywhere in every direction.

XXVI

A Visitor: I look at Swami's photograph on my desk at home in my country and I receive Swami's instructions. He ordered me to come to India for this Conference.

Sai: You think of Sai and get some feeling.

Visitor: I look at Swami's photograph and send Him questions and problems from other people, and I receive His orders and instructions for those people. Is that all right?

Sai: No. It is not all right. For yourself you may ask. But you should not think to place yourself between a devotee and Sai. This is a wrong idea.

A Visitor: What are the 16 points of the Avatar? I have asked and nobody knows.

Sai: The difference between man and Avatar? Man experiences the 15 factors, but he is not their master. They go their own ways. As control starts to be gained, man comes closer to the 16th, the all-knowing Paramatma. The five working organs have to do with talking, taking, walking, rejecting (excretion), and eating. The five sense organs: hearing, touch, sight, taste, smell. The five elements: earth, water, fire, air, space. The 16th factor: The all-knowing Paramatma.

73

H: One sees people breaking coconuts in front of Swami's car as He is departing from Prasanthi Nilayam or Brindavan. What is the significance of this?

Sai: As long as there is water, meaning worldly desire in the nut, and as long as the meat clings to the shell, the nut will grow if planted. As the unplanted nut ages, the water disappears, the meat leaves the shell, and the nut will not grow. The nut is chosen as a symbol because of the three eyes—the two physical eyes and the eye of wisdom (unopened). When the nut is broken, it symbolizes breaking the closed heart and asking the Lord to take the contents. This is 'surrender.' Nothing inside can be concealed and, once the nut is broken, it will never grow again.

XXVII

Sai: Mr. 'X' is a great scholar with various degrees and a lifetime of sadhana in the Himalayas and elsewhere.

H: I suppose degrees are O.K., but the only scholarship of interest to this individual is scholarship in Swami's teachings. It is like locating the greatest deposit of gold in the world. Why work at anything else?

Sai: The mention of gold is important. Deposits of gold are not limited to one place in the world, but gold is found only by certain individuals. God is not limited to one place only. He is everywhere and He may be found at any place by those who are pure of heart. And by that I mean where there is love in the heart.

H: No doubt gold is everyplace, but great treasures of gold are seldom found. It is the same with great springs of water. In Baba, one finds the spring of divine sweetness.

Sai: Waters from springs are often impure. Pure water may be found by digging for it. One person may dig 100 feet and another person may find pure water at 40 feet or at 10 feet. It is the same in the spiritual life. The amount of work needed to find the divine sweetness depends on purity of heart.

H: Is it only by the strength of one's love for God that he comes to union with God? Or, are there other essential factors?

Sai: The most beneficial thing that can happen to a person is that he should draw God's love to himself. His love for God is of less importance, because it is an imperfect mixture of divine and worldly love. The most important action whereby to gain God's love is righteousness, dharma. Spread out on a flat surface there may be gold, silver, copper, iron filings, diamonds, rubies, silks and other things of value. But a magnet pays no attention to all the riches, it selects only the iron filings. It is the same with devotees. God does not select on the basis of wealth. He looks to the purity of heart.

H: Swami speaks of 'facing God.' Please explain.

Sai: When two people face each other, each enters the eye of the other, and they are different only in name and form. Otherwise they are the same. So, it is important to face God directly and be one with Him. That is why one naturally closes the eyes in a temple, so as to use the eye of wisdom instead of the physical eyes.

A Visitor: The word, 'sadhana' is used in so many different places.

Sai: Sadhana is just replacement of the bad tendencies of the mind by the divine attributes of the Atma. Mind has two principal bad characteristics: its tendency to not go straight, but to move obliquely; and its tendency to desire and grasp all objects that it sees. It is compared to the snake, who moves by twisting and who bites all it sees. The mind must go straight to God by facing Him directly.

H: Baba says, 'Why fear when I am here.' That must have a wide and deep meaning. Will Baba speak of it?

Sai: 'I am,' refers to the Atma, who is always everywhere. The Atma is like the lion, without fear. 'Fear,' refers to the body, which is subject to worry, depression, trembling, fear. Body is like a sheep, wavering this way and that way. Body is always looking for information, gathering information, questioning. Whereas, Atma, like the lion, is full of courage and without fear. 'Atma' is God. You are God. God is omnipresent. This 'I' is you. That 'I' is you. You are all.

A Visitor: What is 'jnana'?

Sai: Jnana is ordinary knowledge, knowledge about living in the world. Special knowledge is wisdom. Love is giving and forgiving. Selfishness is getting and forgetting. Love is expansion, and selfishness is contraction.

XXVIII

A Visitor: I see evil on all sides, and am puzzled.

Sai: Here is a banana. The skin is useless to us, so it is regarded as bad. But, if there were no skin, the inside would not be protected. Do not regard anything as bad. If a person has done evil to you and you take it as evil and retaliate, then you also have become bad. But, by remaining good and not regarding others as evil, you gain the right to reform them. If there is a bad smell in the room, and if incense is lighted, the fragrance changes the smell of the room. Bad actions should be met with good deeds and a good viewpoint, and the evil will be changed. The difference between good and bad is a function of time. Food when eaten is good. In time that same food undergoes a change, is excreted, and is called bad. Whereas, truth remains the same and does not change with the passage of time. Therefore, the time sequnce is just imagination.

H: The thought arises that some persons are wholly bad, their crimes are so vicious.

Sai: No person is wholly bad, for God is in every person's heart. A mother and son may fight in Court over property, but the relationship of mother and son remains. Two people who have come to hate each other live in two houses. Each has a picture of Baba over the door. The house represents the body, and Baba's picture represents the God resident in the soul. The body may have to be corrected in its behaviour, and the best way is to attract the person with love. There is absolute good but there is no absolute bad. Bad changes, bad is a distorted aspect of good. But it is not possible when one has the ordinary physical vision to see good and bad as one. Only when one knows the divine spark in oneself and in others, only then one sees good and bad as the same. If one can adopt as an attitude the truth that good only is real, and that all one sees is essentially good, even though distorted, one acquires a great strength. The learned might argue about the world and say that all this is illusion and despair, but they can never hope to live without loving the world. Love is not to be disregarded. The world might seem to be untruth from the material viewpoint; but the world is truth if looked at from the transcendental viewpoint.

H: We are asking Swami about the 'bad' people. How about the poor victim of a vicious action?

Sai: Every one is good, but there are bad actions; action and reaction. In terms of the victims of bad action, everything was exactly right. We see only the present. Baba sees the past also. A four-year-old boy was attacked by robbers for the gold chain around his neck. The robbers blinded the boy so he could not identify them. The boy was crying bitterly that he could not see. The parents also were crying. They came to Baba. In the past life, the boy had been a cruel man who had blinded several people. The boy will continue blind but, as a man, if he starts to consider, understanding that he is blind because of past dark deeds and then sincerely repents his bad tendencies and makes a genuine effort to change himself, praying to God to forgive him, Baba may forgive the karma and restore the eyesight.

H: How should we relate to so-called 'bad' people?

Sai: Keep the body separate from people who give bad food to the senses, even though all are brothers. Let souls be in God, but bodies apart.

H: Often it is very difficult to choose the right action. How may one acquire the ability to make this discrimination?

Sai: Every man has the discrimination to know what is right action and what is wrong action. Wrong action develops guilt feelings. Whereas right action is free and without such fear.

XXIX

H: At times, Swami, sounds are still heard as is usual; but every sound is surrounded by silence, and it is the silence that is heard.

Sai: The silence that surrounds outside sounds is God. Inside that silence is the eternal sound of 'Om.' There is only one sound, and that is 'Om.' Every other sound arises from Om.

H: One is conscious of a force, a strength that rises up in oneself. What is that?

Sai: That life force must be turned to God.

H: How does one direct that force?

Sai: Through faith and love. These must be tended with love and care like tender plants. The bud cannot be forcefully pulled up into a tree.

H: Baba said Ramakrishna Paramahamsa merely touched Vivekananda and transformed him?

Sai: Yes, but it was temporary. After a while it fell away. Vivekananda's strong temper rose again, and he had to work out his own sadhana. What Ramakrishna accomplished was to reverse the trend of Vivekananda's life from downwards into material life, to upward into spiritual sadhana. Without that, Vivekananda would have continued in materialistic life.

H: Can it be said that the reversal given to Vivekananda's life by the touch of Ramakrishna is given to our own lives merely by the darshan of Baba?

Sai: Baba does not do that. He slowly and gradually changes the lives of his devotees. But the change is permanent.

H: How should one listen to Swami when He is in conversation or giving a discourse? That is, Swami's words have so many deep and deeper levels.

Sai: Swami is speaking to you in body, with voice. Listen in the natural way. At length, body and mind drop away, and there is divine, direct understanding.

H: Swami is often heard saying, 'Yes, yes, yes.'

Sai: 'Yes, yes, yes' refers to inner acceptance. Experiences and situations arise in the life of a person. His tendency is to say 'yes' to that which is pleasing, and 'no' if the prospect is otherwise . . . . This is a great mistake. Swami says 'Yes, yes, yes' to everything that comes to him. All is the gift of God. Every experience given by God is good. Through sincere and loving enquiry, that 'good' will be found in every experience. 'Yes, yes, yes' refers to inner acceptance. But there is bad work and good work. Wherever they are, they are real. 'Yes, yes, yes' does not change them. A man locks his valuables in a safe and carries away the key in the belief that he is safe with his safe. But thieves take the safe and break it open. So, one must be sure that he understands the essentials of every situation.

H: All the subtle, inside and outside tasks to be done! Spiritual life seems very difficult.

Sai: Vital to spiritual life is self-confidence, the conviction that one is the Atma. Spiritual life is easy. There are some initial problems, as in learning anything. But it is easy. A bowl turned down remains dry no matter how heavy the rain. Whereas a bowl turned up collects some rain even though the rain is very light. If the heart is turned towards God, some grace will be received. If the interest and devotion is intense, grace will fill the bowl. It is life in the outer world that is endless trouble, whereas spiritual life is easy. The necessary concentration one already has. To be reborn again requires no work. Not to be reborn again requires much work. To gain wealth requires much work. To remain poor requires no work.

XXX

H: When a person is in the waking state, he can observe that the dream experience is a projection of his own mind. Swami says that the waking state is also a dream. But where is the vantage point from which we may observe that the waking state is only a dream?

Sai: One may have a dream that he is a child, that he attends school, makes friends, marries, is a father and has a career; a sequence of events that covers 45 years of his life. The dream may occur at 3:15 a.m. and be over by 3:17 a.m. In two minutes of waking time the dreamer has experienced events that extend through 45 years of dream time. When the waking state is transcended, it also is seen to be a dream, and a lifetime in the waking state has taken only a few moments in the transcendental state. The waking state is seen to be a dream, and the dream state a dream within a dream. The dream state is unreality in truth; the waking state is truth in unreality; and the transcendent state is truth in truth. The 'I' in the dream state is taken to be the body. The 'I' in the waking state is taken to be the mind. The 'I' in the transcendent state is God.

H: But Swami, there is another difference between the dream state and the waking state. In the dream state one does not doubt his reality. Whereas in the waking state there is an extremely strong doubt. In the waking state one cannot believe that he is a real entity; one sees himself as a shadow and not as a real person engaged in activity.

Sai: You see yourself as a shadow; and then there is a change, and you experience yourself as real. Like this, it changes back and forth; the two sides of a coin, the face and the obverse.

H: Yes, it is like that.

Sai: But that is not the typical experience of the waking state. It is a yogic stage due to sadhana. People ordinarily experience the dream state as truth while dreaming, and they experience the waking state as truth while awake. What you experience is qualified monism. In the advaitic state, even the shadow is seen as a reflection of the Divine.

Sai: (to the college boys in the group) It is necessary to understand topics such as this, although they are somewhat difficult to grasp.

Sai: (to Hislop) What is that beneath your shirt?

H: (taking chain from around neck and giving it to Swami) It is the ring that Swami gave me that is now broken.

Sai: (after passing around the ring to the college boys) What do you want?

H: If Swami could repair the ring?

Sai: Only that?

H: Whatever Swami pleases would delight me.

(Sai held the broken ring between thumb and forefinger and blew His breath on the ring. Immediately there was a new ring which he gave to the college boys to pass around. When the ring returned, He took the left hand of Hislop and put the ring on the fourth finger. It was a gold ring of delicate filigree setting. The enamel stone was large and oval with a smiling portrait of Baba on a light blue background.)

Sai: In the world, the metal, the stone, the jeweler are all separate, as is the one who will take the ring. But they must be brought together. Whereas, in the world of Swami, the metal, the stone, the jeweler and the one who will take the ring are all one, and that One is God. In the world, time is needed. But God is beyond time. Immediately the ring is ready.

A Visitor: It would be of interest if Baba would do a large creation.

Sai: Since Swami has taken a body, He has imposed certain proper limitations on himself. Swami has created idols of gold, and could just as easily create a mountain of gold. But then the Government would surround him and let nobody through. But Swami will not separate from His devotees. In Baba's life, as with every Avatar, the first 16 years are characterized by constant leelas, then leelas and teaching up to age 45. From age 45 to 60 the emphasis is almost wholly on teaching. After age 60 there is a change.

XXXI

H: The crucifixion of Christ, the metal figure of Christ on the cross that Swami created; the metal, when strongly magnified, appears to be more or less covered with small bumps. What are they?

Sai: They are blood, knots of blood. The body was in bad condition. It had been hurt and injured over the entire body. At death, the blood came to a sudden stop, and the bumps are clots of blood.

H: Swami, on the photo enlargements of the statue, it also looks as if a sort of slice off the nose had been removed.

Sai: The nose is whole. That is a heavy blood stain. When the face itself is enlarged, it is seen as a dead face. Swami made the metal image of the body after its death.

H: Because of pictures being around, and the story and pictures being in books, the little figure on the cross is becoming quite famous. What should be done with it? Should it be placed in the new Sathya Sai Museum?

Sai: For the museum, Swami will make a big image of Christ. The small one was for you. You keep it.

Sai: What do you make of Christmas?

H: I was never really interested in Christianity, but I have paid more attention since Swami made the crucifix.

Sai: I mean, what does Christmas represent?

H: The birth of Christ is represented.

Sai: The 25th is not the birth. It was on the 24th, near midnight.

H: Not long ago, I found out something very interesting about the Christian religion. The early Christian Fathers of the Eastern Church knew something of which modern Christians have no idea. The early Fathers taught that one should constantly say, 'Lord Jesus Christ, have mercy on me.' There is constant repetition of Christ's name until the Name goes into the heart where the repetition continues without cessation. Along with the repetition of the Name, the form of Christ is visualized in the mind. I learned of this through reading an old book, THE WAY OF THE PILGRIM, translated from the Russian.

Sai: As time goes on, the significant factors of the spiritual path are lost. The Christian mystics took up the repetition of the name of Christ starting about 19 years after his death. As time goes on, human nature comes to the front and the divine is put aside and forgotten. That which was known of the spiritual path after the time of Rama was no longer there at the time of Krishna. And that which Krishna taught was gone when Sai came. It is the same with the Buddhists, the Moslems and the Jains.

H: What the early Christian mystics taught was surely the heart of the Christian religion; and one never hears of it today from Christian people.

Sai: What is your work in America?

H: I am retired and do no work.

Sai: Then how do you pass the days?

H: Mostly the day is spent with Swami. It starts with Swami in the morning and goes through the day. I work at my desk trying to make sense out of my financial affairs, and then there are many tasks in relation to the house. But really, Bhagavan is our life. Our discrimination, added to our direct experience, tells us that Baba is God Himself—so what else is there, what else can there be?

Sai: It is a good opportunity for you to study Sai's teachings.

H: Swami must tell me what He wants the Chairman of the Central Committee of America to do. That will be my work now.

Sai: You will need to do quite a bit of touring, visiting the

Sathya Sai Baba Centers. For this, since you are now retired, you should not pay out of your own pocket.

H: I don't worry much about the money. I am a financial idiot, and it can only be by Sai's grace that I am not 'flat broke' by now! When I visit Centers, Swami, they will expect discourses. About what shall I talk?

Sai: Speak on the principles of spiritual life; on those things that Swami says are essential to reach God. Spiritual life such as discipline, devotion, sadhana. Be clear, do your duty calmly, and the goal will be reached in due course.

H: Swami's teaching is clear enough, and that can be said.

Sai: What is needed most now is that the devotees must have tolerance of each other. And, they do not have any seasoned discrimination in respect to the many 'gurus' and their various spiritual paths. They have not had the face to face confrontation with Swami that you have had. You have considerable background in spiritual life and they have not. You must carry them along with you.

H: The new rules for Centers that will be in the GUIDELINES will shake many Centers.

Sai: That will be the case. Sai Centers must reflect the distinctive character of our organization. There cannot be a mixing of a Sathya Sai Baba Center with the many gurus and the many spiritual paths. We have our goal. Swami has shown the path to follow and we must quietly and sincerely devote ourselves to that path. The leaders must provide the example in their conduct.

H: Not all present Centers devote themselves entirely to the Sai teachings.

Sai: At present, some people form their own organisations and use the Sai Center name as a tool to promote their own interests and ends. Some leaders have yoga business and use the Sai name as a way to add to the business.

H: What do we do about such? Is the prominent leader an exception to the rule; the rule that a leader of a Sai Center

85

cannot carry on yoga classes, or any classes related to spiritual sadhana, and charge the students money?

Sai: Swami is not aware of having exceptions.

H: I understand. The same principle applies to all. Probably such a leader will at once say that entirely apart from their yoga business, they will continue to be an Officer of a Sai Center.

Sai: How would that be practical? There would still be the same mixture. Such individuals will have to decide to go one way or the other. Two ways at once will not do; and that will be the case for everyone. Those devotees who wish to determine a separate path for their organizations are quite free to do so.

H: One leader I know has a dual personality. In some cases, the individual is extremely kind-hearted, and in others, if a devotee crosses the leader in any way, it is 'off with his head,' and he is gone from the scene.

Sai: That is the way of the world. Kindness is used with people. But when people do wrong, they must be corrected sternly. Swami does the same. To those who act according to His command and obey Him, He gives everything to fill their wants and needs. But, if after a long treatment of love and patience they still disobey, Swami gives severe punishment. He gives it because of His love for the person and because He knows that if He does not punish, the person is spoiled.

H: But there is a considerable difference. With Swami, it is God Almighty who punishes. Where in the other case, it is the leader of a Center, a personality, who does the punishing.

Sai: Yes, it is as you say. Sai rewards and punishes without self. When humans reward and punish, there is self-interest.

H: Yes, self-interest is there. When the individual of whom I spoke helped some people in trouble with remarkable generosity, the individual put in a stipulation that on the surface was also generous but which resulted in the people repaying the generosity with much service.

Sai: That was all right. The individual helped the people, and they should show gratitude. Unless a person can show gratitude to another being at his own level, how can he be expected to show gratitude to the divine?

H: To my mind, ingratitude to God is a great sin.

Sai: To fail to show gratitude is wrong. To show ingratitude is a sin. There are four classes of people in the world. First, those who call everything they see as good. Second, those who call wrong as wrong, and good as good. Third, those who do not make a judgment. In each of these three some reason can be seen. The fourth class is those to whom everyone and everything is evil; they do not see any good.

H: There must be just a few people in this fourth class; perhaps from the lower socio-economic group?

Sai: On the contrary. It is the largest class of all. And it is not a special characteristic of poor people. The poorest peasants often rely on our Indian traditions of thousands of years past, and they behave very cautiously. They fear to commit a sin. Poor people who have moved near the cities lose contact with their hereditary background and live in a world which they see as wholly bad. Likewise, the so-called educated middle-class, who are half educated and half ignorant, do not fear sin nor do they believe there is God. They become sinful, corrupt, immoral, greedy, hateful and so on, and that is their world.

H: As Swami says it, I recollect the West and it is true that in the West those who are corrupt are from the educated middle class who gain positions of wealth, authority, and power. But many workers are also corrupt in their lives and their relationships. But in America I do not think the same behavior and attitude is typical of the upper class.

Sai: If by upper class you mean those who have a tradition and who are correctly trained by their parents, then the same would be true even of a large number of farmers living in Indian villages.

XXXII

A Visitor: Swami, Mr. 'X' wishes to make a film about the so-called 'lost years of Jesus.' He has much experience in making films and he is a Sai devotee.

Sai: Jesus realized that he was Christ in his 25th year. For eight years following his 16th birthday, he travelled in India, Tibet, Iran, and Russia. He was variously regarded as a beggar or as a sanyasi. Jesus had no money. His parents were very poor and practically abandoned him at an early age.

H: What is the art of looking whereby one may see the Lord even in unpleasant and disagreeable persons?

Sai: Even in persons of unpleasant nature, be aware that the Lord is in the heart even of that person. Have that aspect in mind and treat the person from that viewpoint to the best of your ability. In time that person will respond and his nature will change. One sees people as good or bad because he does not see the person in full, but only one-sided. Suppose a mother were six feet tall and her young child could not as yet walk, but could only sit on the floor. Will that mother say, 'I am six feet tall and I stand erect. I will not bend myself for the sake of the child'? Or, does she bend down to the child because of her love for the child? As another example, there may be a person of many big degrees who is with small children; will he refuse to help the children because he knows so much? The children must start to learn by being drilled in the A B C's. They must learn at their level.

H: Eyes see body. How does one see God Himself?

Sai: In order to see the moon, does one need a torch? It is by the light of the moon that one sees the moon. In like fashion, if one wishes to see God, it is by love, which is the light of God, that one may see Him.

H: Swami says that like the blind man who has no eyes to see, we are likewise blind and unable to see our own divinity. With what vision does one see his own divinity?

Sai: A blind man cannot see his body. You can, because

you have eyes. But you have no eyes to see your spiritual body. You have a spiritual body that is omnipresent. That body can be seen with the spiritual eye.

H: Would Swami describe the spiritual eye?

Sai: Oh, yes. The spiritual eye is God. Attain Him and the spiritual eye will open.

H: What does Swami mean when he says 'To look within oneself'? What is meant by 'look'?

Sai: 'Looking within' does not mean looking into the body of flesh and bones. It means transcending the senses, as in deep meditation.

H: As one turns inward, he encounters feeling. Women talk of the heart. Swami puts emphasis on the heart. What is meant by the word, 'heart'?

Sai: 'Heart' is the inside. 'Art' is outside. Heart is inside.

H: Swami says that 'the heart is the reflection of the Atma.' And also that 'the heart is the best mirror for reflecting truth.' What is that 'heart'? What does Swami refer to?

Sai: Heart is the consciousness.

H: Is the 'heart' that women talk about, the same as what Swami means?

Sai: No. That is the subconscious mind mixed up with their desire.

H: Just under my skin, about an inch, there seems to be a mirror. When I see Baba outside, I also see Him in that 'mirror.' The 'mirror' reflects Baba's every move. Of these two, the Baba I see with my two eyes, and the Baba of the inside reflection, which is the most real?

Sai: Consciousness is a reflection. If pure, it is a clear reflection. It is by the sankalpa of Baba that the reflection is seen.

H: Is it to the 'inside' Baba that prayers and devotion should be addressed?

Sai: When Baba is found within, he will be seen everywhere outside.

H: When one enquires within, 'I' is found to be 'I.' That 'I' is thought to be oneself. But then, it seems to me that 'I' is not me at all, but is Baba.

Sai: That is correct; 'I' is Baba. Have no doubt. You and Baba are one. Not the tendencies and so on, but the essential 'you' and Baba are one and the same. 'I' is Baba.

H: Some say it is necessary to mortify the body to overcome the tendencies?

Sai: Some spiritual aspirants do tapas and various austerities that torture and weaken the body. This is wrong. If there is a healthy body, this is the base for healthy thoughts.

H: One's tendencies are there for a long time. Despite oneself, they come up again and again.

Sai: There is the sun, the magnifying glass, and the paper. God is the sun, far away. The heart is the glass, the desires and tendencies, the paper. If the glass is just right, the paper is burned at once. If the heart has strong love for God, and faith in Him, the glass is automatically right.

H: One very strong tendency is in the tongue, the problem of taste, which gives rise to craving for more. How do we overcome that?

Sai: The body is like a boil. Water is for cleansing the wound. Food is the medicine. Clothing is the bandage. Considering the body so, reduces the strength of taste. But what is taken in by seeing, hearing, talking, is the more important food. Gross food for the body is like digging a well. Whereas pure, subtle impressions taken in by the other senses is like building a wall high into the heavens. It is building the wall high that should have the major emphasis.

H: The body is like a boil. But Swami often uses the phrase, 'body is the temple of God.'

Sai: In the spiritual world, there is a different arithmetic: 3−1=1. There is you, the mirror, and the image. Remove the mirror, and there is only one left. Life is the mirror, body is the reflection. Be attached to God, and there is only One, God. The body is the temple of God. The life of the person is the priest. The five senses are the vessels used in the religious ceremony.

90

Atma is God, the idol of God. One cannot say that the body is the temple of God unless it is. Every act, thought and word should be worship in the temple. The five senses should constantly be cleansed and polished, so that the worship is reverently offered to God. One goes to the office and says to himself that every act of the day should be worship of God, and it will be so.

H: Swami says that when the senses leave their place and mix with worldly objects, pain and pleasure are produced. What is the proper place of the senses?

Sai: It is all the play of desire. Desire for worldly objects produces pleasure and pain, whereas desire for God confers bliss and does not produce pain.

H: But Swami, most of our actions arise from worldly desires. We see, hear, think, feel, smell. Then there is some desire and that leads to action.

Sai: God works through you as desire.

H: Swami! Does God prompt even the bad desire?

Sai: There is the strong thrust of life force, the desire to live. If it goes into action in a favorable field, it becomes love; otherwise, it remains as desire. If desire is expressed in a favorable field, it is expressed as love. Then knowledge arises; then bliss. The force, the strength, the energy, the motivation in desire is God. Whether the desire is good or bad is related to time, place and person. In early years, a desire for worldly achievement might be good. In later years, the same desire might be bad. Fruit that is good one day may be rotten several days later. One side of an apple may become good, the other side rotten. Discrimination says eat the good side and discard the bad. There is another force in you through which God works, and that is discrimination. That force must be used to put aside wrong action. The power of discrimination knows what is right and what is wrong. The wrong desire is God overshadowed by Maya, whereas discrimination is God less overshadowed by Maya.

H: Swami! This really explains the whole problem of good and evil.

Sai: Yes. The story of Valmiki is an illustration. He was a ruthless killer and robber without any doubt about his actions. He, at one time, listened to the five sages, and started repeating 'Ram.' The same strength and force that made him a terrible criminal was turned to Godly desire and action, and he gained God-realization. 'Rama' started to be repeated by Valmiki and, gaining speed, became jumbled up with 'Ma' and 'Mara.' In this he lost body sense and transcended the senses. Losing body sense should be like that, natural and not forced.

XXXIII

H: Swami says that body, mind and intelligence do not work for anybody, that they do their own work. What does that mean?

Sai: What is meant is, 'unfortunately, that is the case.' They are doing their own work, but the work should be co-ordinated for the benefit of the higher. For example, the eyes see. Seeing is their work. But unless they see for somebody there is no point in their work. The mind should be seeing through the eyes. The intelligence should be directing and controlling the mind, for that is the 'own work' of intelligence.

H: Then, for whom should the entire mechanism be functioning?

Sai: For the Atma. A small example: The earth turns on its own axis, but at the same time it is revolving around the sun. The various faculties of man should do their own work, but the Atma is the center of their universe.

H: There seems to be something wrong. The Atma is not doing its work of directing the faculties. How can one bring the faculties under the control of the Atma?

Sai: When one realizes that the Atma is the reality,

everything will function very smoothly. It is a question of surrendering all to the Atma.

H: But Swami has said that one cannot surrender that which he really does not own and of which he is not in control.

Sai: It is not a question of surrendering or giving to some other one. One surrenders to oneself. Recognition that the Atma is oneself is surrender. Surrender really means the realization that all is God, that there is nobody who surrenders, that there is nothing to be surrendered, nor is there anyone to accept a surrender. All is God. There is only God.

H: 'Surrender' is not really a very good word. It quite fails to convey what is meant.

Sai: 'Surrender' is world language. To correctly describe it, language of the divine is needed. There is no adequate word in the English language, therefore the use of 'surrender' goes on.

XXXIV

H: When Swami says, 'The form of the Lord,' what does He mean? That is, when I think of the Lord, the image of Baba comes to mind and that is only natural. But beyond that, what?

Sai: If you continue to visualize the Form when you are engaged in activity, you will make mistakes. For instance, if you try to visualize the Lord when you are working in the office, you make mistakes. So, when engaged in action, 'Visualizing the Lord' means doing the work in God's name, and not doing the work to gain the fruit of the work.

H: Well then, about the Name, repeating the Name?

Sai: When God comes taking a human form, it is very difficult to see Him as the Lord. One sees that body, then one's own body, and one cannot but relate the two and put that body at the same level as oneself. But if the Lord came in all His majesty, people would be afraid and would have no opportunity to know and love the Lord. For example, people worship an image of a snake in a temple, hoping that the worship will bring the birth of a child. But if the snake became alive and wriggled across the floor towards them, they would take to their heels. People could not stand the Lord in super-human form. It is only when the Lord comes in human body that people are able to approach Him and learn to love Him and know Him even a little bit. But one should not make the mistake of thinking that is all there is to the Lord. For instance, the airplane flying high in the sky descends to the airport. But one should not make the mistake of thinking that the plane is a ground machine because they see it on the ground. Once it has taken on its load of passengers, it again zooms up high into the sky. In like fashion, although the Lord has made a landing here on earth, so to speak, He is not limited by His human form.

H: May Swami please tell us more about saying the name of God?

Sai: Here is a small example. A man had to pass through 20 miles of forest at night, and he had only a small lantern and started to cry, for he could see for only three feet. Some travelers came along and asked the reason for his sorrow. They exclaimed, 'But sir, when you walk, carrying the lamp with you, if you can see only two feet ahead of you it is enough, and you could travel in that way through a hundred miles of dark forest without trouble. But if you leave the lantern where it is, you cannot move at all in this dark forest.' In the same way, the name of the Lord may be written in the book you are looking at, but you may find your way only by using the Name. The Name should be woven into the breath so that you are calling on Him all day long. Sohum—'He am I.' 'He' with the in-breath; 'I' with the out-breath. Or Sai Ram. Or the name of your choice, said with the movement of the breath. Breath is form; thus the name and the form go together. Breath is life. Life is God. Breath is God; the name of God and the form of God. Breathe God. See God. Eat God. Love God. The name of God will illumine every step of your life and take you to Him. The name must be said with love. God is love. If breath is said with love, then life is love. There is no shakthi stronger than love. If it is said with love, the name of God, any name of God—Ram, Sai Ram, Krishna, Jesus, Sohum—that small name will open up and illuminate the whole of life. For the one who desires to realize God, only the Name is needed. The ocean is vast, but a huge steamship is not needed to go on the ocean. Just a small tire will take one on the ocean.

H: In respect to repetition of the name of the Lord, what is the relationship between Sai Baba, Sai Ram, Sohum? And which form is to be visualized for each?

Sai: Sai Baba is the physical form. Sai Baba also means Divine Father and Mother. The syllable 'Sa' means divine. The syllable 'ai' means mother. Baba is the word for father. 'Sai Baba,' therefore, means Divine Mother and Father. Sai Ram represents the same form as Sai Baba. Sohum does not have a form. It means, 'I am God.' Just as a person has several names but they refer to the same body. The repetition of name with form is at the beginning. Later on one worships the omnipresent transcendent divine. If one sees God as the essence of every person he meets, it is also appropriate to love Sai Ram constantly in the mind, because then the diverse forms merge into the Sai Ram form.

H: What is the correct way to chant 'OM'?

Sai: The sound of 'OM' is 'A U M.' 'A' starts softly from the throat. It is the earth. 'U' comes from the mouth and the sound rises in volume. 'M' is sounded with the lips, with decreasing volume. Like a plane, heard distantly, increasing in sound as it approaches and fading with distance. 'A' is the world. 'U' is heaven. 'M' is divine, beyond all the senses.

H: Suppose one fails to achieve this perfect pronunciation?

Sai: The perfect OM is not too important if there is love. Love is the bond of devotion between mother and child, and if child cries, mother does not worry if the cry is discordant. She rushes to the child and cares for him. Divine Mother is every place. Swami is here, but divine Mother is everywhere. So, everybody has a chance. As soon as a person starts to yearn for God, divine Mother is there to respond with grace. In all these matters, love is vital. Devotion to God means love of God. The real OM is spontaneous; it enters through the two nostrils, up to the forehead center and out through the ears to the world; like the broadcast from a radio tower.

H: Is not OM a dangerous sound to use? I have heard that the OM sound is continuous, and continuously sustains the universe. Whereas man breaks the continuity of his saying 'OM' and so his life is likewise broken. I have heard of a number of such instances, and it is said that OM is suitable only for sanyasis who have already broken their worldly ties.

Sai: What is a sanyasi? There are three types. First is 'cloth sanyasi' who pretends renunciation by wearing an ochre robe. There are thousands of such in India. Next is the 'sense sanyasi' who gains control of his senses. These persons should never leave the world for solitude. They should remain in life where they may watch their reactions and know if their sense control is genuine. Then there is he who has surrendered to the Lord, dedicating the fruit of every action to Him. In this sanyasi, ego has no place. His heart is pure. His senses become calm and are not affected by the opposites. If the heart is pure, then the continuity of the 'OM' sound will not be broken. And, if something that seems bad does arise, then it is unreal, for only OM is real.

H: Swami says that people make a mistake by not saying 'Sohum' with every breath. How does one do it?

Sai: 'Saa' is He. 'Hum' is I. Yogi 'X' whom you mentioned, teaches to say 'Saa Saa' 24 hours each day. Since 'Hum' is not said, the 'I,' the personality, is supposed to subside. It is extremely difficult to do it 24 hours a day, and in sleep it is almost impossible. Yogi 'X' says he does it, but he does not. What is the use of struggling with a very difficult practice like that, when there is an easier, more effective way?

H: Well, Swami, putting Yogi 'X' aside, I want to do as Baba says, and say 'Sohum' with every breath. What is the technique? Is it said with each breath?

Sai: The breath is always saying 'Sohum.' The practice is to say 'So' with every in-breath, and 'Hum' with the out-breath. Say it in thought. It is intended to keep the mind fixed and quiet. After a while it becomes automatic. During the day say 'Sohum.' At night, during sleep, the sound naturally changes to OM.

H: Should one think, 'He am I'?

Sai: No. The sound is 'Sohum.' It is not an Indian word or an American word. It is the sound of what the breath is saying. Of course, it is all right to appreciate the meaning of the sound.

H: Swami says that 'Sohum' is the natural sound of the breath. Listening to my breath, it does not seem to me that I hear the sound of breath in that way.

Sai: Sound through nose and mouth are mixed with mind or idea, and may be heard in various ways. The fact is, that when the mind is without movement and the breath is perfectly spontaneous and natural, the sound of that breath (through the nostrils) is 'Sohum.' Breath through the mouth goes into the stomach.

H: Krishna told Arjuna to sound OM in the mind.

Sai: OM is every place, in mind, tongue, heart, etc. First sound OM on the tongue and then in the mind. The sounding of OM 21 times is important: five outer senses, five inner senses, five lives (the five elements), five sheaths (the kosas), and the Jiva.

XXXV

A Visitor: How does one surrender to God and to life?

Sai: Surrender to God and to life means the absence of duality and being of the same nature as God. But such a state is beyond man's will. Surrender is when doer, deed, and object are all God. It cannot be forced. It comes naturally to a heart filled with love for God. God is as a spring of fresh and sweet water in the heart. The best tool to dig a well to that inexhaustible source and savour its sweetness is Japa, the repetition of the name of the Lord. Dedicate every action to the Lord and there will be no place for ego. That is the quickest way for the ego to subside.

A Visitor: How does one progress fast on the path?

Sai: Love is the path. Start the day with love. Spend the day with love. Fill the day with love. End the day with love. This is the way to God; expansion love, not contraction and selfishness, not 'my.' Such practices as meditation, japa, mantra, bhajan are like soap. Without water, soap is not of use. The water is likened to love. It is the water that is important. Without love you live in death. Love is life. All are one; be alike to everyone. Enquiry is of great importance. Who am I? Body? No. House? No. 'I' am 'I'; that is the truth. The body is like a water bubble. The mind is like a mad monkey. The mind is worse, it has no reason and season; even a monkey has this.

A Visitor: Is it all right to say 'Sai Ram'?

Sai: 'Sa' means divine. 'Ai' means mother. 'Ram' means He who is in the heart as pure delight. Sai Ram means Divine Mother and Father. Sohum, Sai Ram, Sivoham, Sambasiva, all mean the same.

A Visitor: Baba, I am so tired. I am without energy. How may I get energy?

Sai: Energy arises from surrender to God.

A Visitor: Would it be all right for me to go for a reading from the book of Brighu?

Sai: That is not Swami's business whether you go or not. What is written is true, but the interpretation is faulty.

Visitor: Baba, my energy?

Sai: Energy comes from the heart expanding. A small, closed heart—no energy. If Baba is known in the heart, then the heart expands. Body is the temple. Heart is the seat. God is installed there.

A Visitor: Are you satisfied?

Sai: I am always happy. Love is my form. Always happy. Sometimes to correct a situation, the sound of Swami's voice may change, but inside there is no anger.

H: Swami, excuse me. A person observing Swami moving amongst people, and choosing some of them for special attention or interview, is puzzled why some are chosen and why some are not.

Sai: Yes, it is quite natural that you are puzzled. One looking from the outside cannot know who is worthy and who is not.

H: Swami says that one should not speak of the Lord with those who are not devotees. What are the implications?

Sai: It is all right to speak to a group. The leaders will become interested and they, in turn, will tell their followers. But to engage in individual private conversations with those who have no faith will just result in argument and discussion and will be a waste of time.

H: Each devotee is so anxious to touch Swami's feet. What is the meaning of touching the feet?

Sai: God is positive. Man is negative. If contact is made, the divine current flows from positive to negative. For this reason the Indian tradition of touching a divine person. But without some form of discipline and limitation, people would be touching face and body. Hence, the custom of touching the lotus feet.

H: Swami says, 'keep water out of the boat.' How is that done?

Sai: How can one keep water out of the boat of one's life? Turn fully to God and there is no boat, no boat is needed. God is every place. The connection to Him is inside, in the heart.

XXXVI

H: Must a certain length of time pass before liberation?

Sai: The time needed for liberation is like this. Somebody asks, how long do you need to eat? The answer may be, 'Five minutes to half an hour.' It is the wrong answer. It will take as long to eat as needed to fill the stomach.

H: Is there naturally a desire for liberation in man?

Sai: Sadhana does not bring liberation. It only calms and controls the rajasic and thamasic gunas. The sathwic guna has always the liberation desire. When the sathwic guna in man is in control, liberation comes.

H: In the West, sadhana is generally taken to be a process of self-improvement. But does that imply identification with the changing personality?

Sai: First there may be the urge to self-improvement. Moral nature and character may be seen to need improvement. But the next stage is enquiry; enquiry into the reality of this and that. Seven tenths (7/10) of sadhana is enquiry. 'I' as generally used by people, refers to the body.

H: Mahayana Buddhism says that one has the choice to merge or not, even at the last moment before final liberation.

Sai: The choice of merging or of rebirth upon the dawn of freedom rests with the wish. There is no selfishness in the wish to merge in God. It is not contraction, it is expansion.

XXXVII

(A Visitor, a prince from another state of India, came to Bhagavan, offered some acres of land for a yoga center and asked that Bhagavan please visit his state and use his will to avert the danger of political violence.)

Sai, to the Visitor: Swami's love is the same for all, even for those who engage in bad actions. These suffer, not because of Swami's anger, but because only through suffering do their minds turn inward in self-enquiry. And only through self-enquiry will they be free of the illusion that separates them from God. The only gift acceptable to Swami is the heart. Acres of land are of no interest to Him. Presently, there is great disorder amongst both politicians and students. This will continue for a time, but at a certain point Swami will step in and bring about some order.

H: How about order in America and Europe?

Sai: Countries are like carriages. The engine is God. The first carriage is India. The other carriages will follow. According to the astrology of ancient times, the change in world conditions to be brought about by Swami's influence will come in about 15 years (this conversation was in December, 1968). This was predicted 5,600 years ago in the Upanishads. The coming of Baba, the Sai Avatar, which includes the three incarnations, is all forecast quite clearly. People born in this present generation may consider themselves quite fortunate.

XXXVIII

H: Is today's world without saints who have direct and deep God experience?

Sai: There are people, even today, who have the genuine experience of divine vision and self-realization. But they do not travel here and there in the world, building up a following of disciples. They stay very quietly away from public view and do sadhana. If you were to find such a one and ask for guidance, he would not be interested in you. If the life of a 'guru' who is out in the world is closely examined, it will be found that he has desires and problems. His knowledge is from books and other persons and he has no full and real experience of the divine of whom he speaks. Such persons are caught in the bog of samsara, just as you are. How can they pull you to firm ground? Nowadays, God is the only genuine guru. Call on Him and He will guide you. He is in your heart, ever ready to help, protect and guide you.

H: Swami says that these are people who have divine vision. How can one achieve that vision?

Sai: Divine vision erases from the mind the seeing of that which is impermanent. Name, form and characteristics will in time disappear. So why wait? Erase them from the vision now. Erase them from the mind now and see only that which is real.

Why bother about the illusion, that which disappears? Far better to give one's time and attention to reality. Divine vision is seeing through the ephemeral illusion and abiding in and with the reality. God is the eternal reality. He is the changeless basis of every phenomenon. King Janaka became firmly established in the divine vision. Name, form, personality, attributes had been so thoroughly seen through that they never again came into his vision during the balance of his lifetime. Divine vision is the result of practice and of God's grace. At times, divine vision may appear to arise spontaneously, but it is because of work done by the person in a previous life.

H: What is the difference between a person of divine vision and a person who is fully God-realized?

Sai: There is a difference. The God-realized person, the Jivanmukta, no longer has any identification whatsoever with the body. He is one in whom only the divine vision is active. He pays no attention to the body, and it wastes away and dries up. He does not bother with food and water. They do not even come to mind. As a result, 21 days is the time that life can remain in the body under these circumstances. He has lost all body identification and neither eats nor drinks except as force-fed. The 21 days may vary a little due to the condition of the person. King Janaka retired to the forest and became a jivanmukta. Life remained in his body for 19 days. The person of divine vision is known as a raja yogi. He retains some body identification, and thus continues to live with the body. King Janaka reigned for many years as a raja yogi. Jivanmukti is permanent God-realization. It is merging with God. There can be a temporary God-realization for a few hours or a day or so in deep meditation, or at various levels of samadhi, but that is not permanent. It is not merging.

H: Sorry, Swami, divine vision is still not clearly understood.

Sai: There is a piece of clear glass. From one side one can look through and see the object on the other side. If the clear glass is plated with a silver film on one side, it becomes a mirror in which one may see himself, and objects on the other side of the mirror are not seen. Likewise, through consciousness one may see the outside sensory world. Or, with his intelligence, he may look to and become aware of that which may be found within himself. If one lives and keeps himself within the reality found within, with Godly thoughts, desires, and interests, if one keeps his life centered on the Godly side of consciousness, the consciousness becomes a mirror coated on its outer surface with the dust of the sensory world. On the pure inward surface of this mirror, on the pure mind and the pure heart, one may see the reality of himself reflected and this constitutes self-realization. That is raja yoga. King Janaka became one who lived his life in this way.

H: Swami, even perfect men seem to have troubles.

Sai: Various saints (Swami mentioned some names) had endless troubles in their lives with family, harsh treatment from others, and so on. But their faith in God remained untouched.

H: But Swami, since these men were already purified saints, why did suffering and troubles continue for them?

Sai: They themselves did not suffer. Jesus did not suffer. But it was necessary that they go through what is generally regarded as suffering so the world could have noble examples of worldly detachment and unshakeable faith in God.

H: In the scriptures there are a number of stories about very great sages who had very big tempers. How could that be?

Sai: The angry sages of the scriptures were in error in their sadhana. Their reactions were rajasic. The sathwic sadhanas are best; they give trouble to nobody.

H: When reading, I found a passage saying that sage Viswamitra created a duplicate universe. Could such a thing be possible?

Sai: Yes. The sage agreed to transport one of his disciples to the heavenly regions with the disciple remaining in his physical body. The gods did not agree. Viswamitra became very angry and created a universe, even though God came to him and asked him not to. Viswamitra created even a pantheon of gods in the subtle space and then transported his disciple there in body. But that which is contrary to God's will cannot last, and Viswamitra's universe did not endure.

H: Prahlada was not fully God-realized since his body continued to live. How could he, therefore, be so firmly established in the Atma that he could endure extreme torture with a smile?

Sai: Prahlada was a special case, created by God as an example of perfect faith in the name of God, an absolute unchanging faith that God was in all things, even inanimate pillars and idols. Prahlada felt no pain during his torture. Because of his perfect faith that God would come when called, God blocked out all pain.

H: One would greatly wish to see God only.

Sai: It is not that one takes every object in the world and changes it into God. One is not able to do that. It is not possible, is it, to take nature and all objects and make them one shade of color? But if one puts on glasses of a certain color, then everything is seen in that color. One is able to change his eyes so that everything he sees is that 'one color,' God.

H: Swami says that all should be seen as God. Should one also see his wife as God?

Sai: Wife should not be seen as God. If so seen, she will sit on your head. She should be treated as wife. And God should be seen as her inner reality.

XXXIX

A Visitor: These miracles that Swami does by moving His hand and out come very costly things from nowhere. Is there some explanation?

Sai: Some objects, Swami creates in just the same way that he created the material universe. Other objects, such as watches, are brought from existing supplies. There are no invisible beings helping Swami to bring things. His sankalpa, his divine will brings the object in a moment. Swami is everywhere. His creations belong to the natural unlimited power of God and are in no sense the product of yogic powers as with yogis or of magic as with magicians. The creative power is in no way contrived or developed, but is natural only.

H: Is it true that wild animals will not harm a saintly person?

Sai: There was once a guru who told his disciple that God was in everything. The disciple believed the statement. That very day there was a royal parade. The king was the center of attraction riding on an enormous elephant. Ignoring the rules of safety for such parades, the disciple planted himself firmly in the path of the royal elephant, and he paid no attention to the cries of warning that he would be trampled to death. Upon reaching him, the elephant lifted him and put him safely to one side. The disciple went to the guru and complained that although God was in both the elephant and himself, he had been unable to remove the elephant from his path. That on the contrary, the elephant had removed him. The guru explained that it was merely a matter of the elephant having greater physical strength. He told the disciple that had he not been looking at God in the elephant the beast would have killed him just as a matter of ordinary work. However, since the disciple was looking at God in the elephant, God had safely lifted him out of harm's way. No animal, not even a cobra, will harm the person who sees God as the essential reality of the animal or the snake. The same is usually true as regards dangerous men, but there are some exceptions here because of karmic implications.

XL

H: I bought this book, TEN SAINTS OF INDA.

Sai: (opening the book and looking at the names) They are not saints. They were scholars and heads of religious sects. (Sai read through the lists making a comment in Telugu about each name. Translator was silent.)

H: Swami, it would be good to know the names of some real saints so that I could read about them.

Sai: What is meant by 'saint'?

H: I guess I mean a messenger from God. From the list of ten names, the world thinks of Sankara, Ramakrishna, and Ramana Maharshi as being such.

Sai: Ramakrishna started as a devotee of God. There was Mother Kali and himself. They were separate. A duality existed. At one point he engaged in a certain action, and Mother Kali never appeared to him again. Towards the end he merged in God and was God-realized.

H: Sankara and Ramana Maharshi were similar cases?

Sai: Yes.

H: Perhaps Buddha was a messenger of God?

Sai: Buddha never mentioned God. The story is known that he was a prince with wife and child, that when he saw misery and death he determined to find their cause. For years he engaged in severe austerities. He made three announcements: All is suffering. All is transient. All is void.

H: Then Buddha did not realize God but realized nirvana?

Sai: Yes. (On a previous occasion Sai had said that one found that for which he sought, and that Buddha had searched for the cause of sorrow.) There is only one yoga, and that is bhakthi yoga. All the others, kriya yoga, hatha yoga, the so-called Sai yoga, pranayama, all the methods and techniques known as yogas belong to the body. They are like drill exercises. Right! Left! Up! Down! Where is the result? They are worthless and a waste of time. Bhakthi yoga is the direct path to God. It is the easy way. All others are useless. There are six types of bhakthi. Madhura means sweet. This is the highest type.

H: What makes madhura the highest?

Sai: In this the devotee sees everything as God. When Jayadeva would lift his clothes to put on, he would see Krishna in the garments and would not treat them as clothes. He would go about the streets unclothed and people would put a garment around him. He would talk with Krishna, sing to Krishna, dance with Krishna, merge with Krishna and fall senseless. He was the guru of Chaitanya.

H: Swami, the description sounds somewhat like Ramakrishna Paramahamsa.

Sai: Jayadeva, Chaitanya, and Ramakrishna are in this madhura stream of bhakthi. Jayadeva saw himself as the bride of Krishna, and because of this, his songs with a worldly meaning, are taken by the public as being lustful. Whereas, the true meanings, the meanings they had for Jayadeva are quite different. To himself, the heart was the bride. He was the Atma.

H: What kind of person was Chaitanya?

Sai: Chaitanya also would sing to Krishna and dance in ecstasy with Krishna. Once he visited an admirer. He was lodged in a room next to the prayer hall. Whenever food was offered to the 5-metal idol of Krishna, Chaitanya was observed to be eating that same food in his room. The host decided to make a test. He locked Chaitanya in his room and there was some opening through which he could see Chaitanya. Food was offered to the Krishna idol, and Chaitanya was seen to be eating food. The host entered the room and slapped Chaitanya on both cheeks. Upon this, the metal idol of Krishna disappeared. This caused great worry, and prayers were made to Krishna. Krishna appeared to the devotees and said, 'You offered food to me and then slapped me when I ate. So I went away.'

H: His devotion had . . . .

Sai: Chaitanya had Sachananda as a guru at one time. The guru wanted to test the devotion of Chaitanya. He placed a cube of sugar on Chaitanya's tongue and said to keep it there until he returned from the river. At the river, Sachananda bathed, washed clothes, did his singing and was away some two hours. On returning, he found Chaitanya with his mouth still open and the cube of sugar vibrating somewhat, but intact on the tongue without any melting. Realizing Chaitanya's greatness, and that his control of the senses was so complete, he prostrated and declared that Chaitanya was his guru.

H: Swami, are there such complete devotees living today, such as Jayadeva and Chaitanya?

Sai: Oh yes. There are. But mostly they contain the devotion within themselves. Sometimes it shows and the world judges the person to be of unsound mind. Swami has encountered such devotees, but he does not grant interviews. But the people live filled with joy. There was one such, a rani, a queen, who was encountered a few years ago. It was not appropriate to the situation to grant an interview.

H: Is it possible for a western person to be such a great bhaktha?

Sai: Oh yes. Quite possible.

H: But Swami, for an office holder who has Swami's work to do in the world, which is the best bhakthi?

Sai: The same.

H: But how could one do work if he were like that?

Sai: It is quite possible to do work and at the same time be the highest bhaktha. It is the feeling that is important, not the work. Even in the case of Jayadeva and Chaitanya, their influence was widespread.

H: Swami, it seems to be the case that from the time of Krishna to Sathya Sai there has been no opportunity . . . .

Sai (interrupting): Time? I am Krishna! Where is time?

H: Swami, I mean between the time of the Krishna body and the Sathya Sai body there has been no opportunity to have God Himself as one's guru.

Sai: Until the Shirdi body.

H: Then, Swami, this has to be the best time of the world for persons to be born?

Sai: Yes. The very best time. Even better than during the lifetime of the Krishna body.

108

XLI

Sai: Cancer. It develops often from a small pustule. There is inflammation, some gas, and from this cancer develops.

H: Swami can cure even terminal cases of cancer?

Sai: Oh yes. A certain person, whom you know, is a good example of that. She was filled with cancer. The doctors gave up, removed tubes, sewed up incisions, and left her only a few days to live. Now she is strong and healthy and works all day.

H: Swami does that only when the karma is appropriate?

Sai: No. If Swami is pleased with the person, he heals that person at once. Karma can have no effect on that.

H: This is extremely important information. Because, when people fail to get cured by Swami, they put it down to the fact that their karma is not ready.

Sai: If the person has a pure heart, and is living Swami's teachings, Swami's grace is automatic. No karma can prevent that.

H: There is a situation in California where a healer wishes to join a Sri Sathya Sai Center and use his healing powers for the benefit of Baba's devotees. The leader of that particular center has had relief from illness by means of the power flowing from the hands of the healer, and has the idea that the healer has been sent by Baba and that Baba is doing the healing through the person of the healer. I was requested to ask Swami for His viewpoint.

Sai: The power flowing from the healer is not Swami's power. It is evil power. The healer is himself in need of healing. Divine power is everyplace; it arises from within. Both these bodies (pointing to Hislop and the driver of the car) are strong and healthy (implying that the health was due to divine power without the agency of an outside healer).

H: The healer also has a question. He asks if what he is doing is all right.

Sai: No. It is not all right. It is not divine power flowing through the person of the healer.

H: How then should one be healed?

Sai: By ordinary medical means and by prayer.

H: But Swami, there are thousands of cases around the world of sick people being healed by healers. What about them?

Sai: Any benefit is only a temporary feeling of relief and is not real. If a healing occurs, it is because the person has had a feeling or thought of God.

H: Then power from God does not flow into a person?

Sai: Where is God? He is within you. From within He heals.

A Visitor: Baba, since time is simply your will and has no reality outside of that, and duration of time also being your will, why not shorten time a bit? People have so much suffering, why do they have to suffer for so long a time?

Sai: They are being tested, but it should not be called so. It is grace. Those who suffer have my grace. Only through suffering will they be persuaded to turn inward and make the enquiry. And without turning inward and making enquiry, they can never escape misery.

H: People have said they are being punished by Swami. Is this a fact?

Sai: Of course. In punishing a person for misdemeanor, Swami punishes in order to correct the defaulter. But, though harsh in appearance and voice, Baba is all love inside. Sometimes Swami corrects a person in private, at other times in public. It depends on the individual. If the correction is in public, then all who hear may learn what pleases Swami and what displeases him. Butter may be cut with a finger, but a rock needs an iron hammer. It all depends on the material, the person. Swami is very strict in his rules and principles. An Avatar does not compromise. To the devotee, strictness is ultimately the best kindness. Depending on the situation, Swami can be soft, kind, or he can be as hard as a diamond. He does not give only one chance, he forgives a thousand times. But if the person still pays no attention, he clips them.

H: Yes, Swami. People, devotees near Swami have to do their best to be perfect in their behavior.

Sai: People, those outwardly 'distant' from Swami, He tells, but not so severely as those 'near'. People judge Swami by his 'near' devotees and so these individuals must follow very strict standards of behaviour. 'Punishment' also depends on the nature and magnitude of the error.

H: Can it be correct, that God forgives sin?

Sai: With sincere repentance all sin can be washed away. God's grace responds. If it is His wish to forgive, nothing can stand in the way. All karma is cancelled out. At the root of all spiritual action—which is without reaction—is the seed of love. If that seed be nourished, it will grow as the tree grows, and all things of value automatically come from that tree of love. Regardless of the sins of the past, if there is deep repentance and love of God, the sins are washed out and the nature purified. To fear otherwise is weakness. God has infinite compassion. Seek His love, and forgiveness follows.

H: Does God forgive even present karma?

Sai: There are three types of karma: past, present and future. Present karma must continue. It is like the carriage behind which is a trail of dust. If the carriage stops, the dust will settle on it. A doubt might be that the carriage cannot forever continue so as to be ahead of its dust. But the carriage need not always travel on a dusty road. It can get on the surfaced highway where there is no dust. The highway is equivalent to the grace of God. There is a difference between the benefit of grace and the benefit of bhakthi, of devotion. A patient with a pain is given a sedative which dulls the pain. But grace is an operation that does entirely away with the pain. Make no mistake, grace does entirely away with karma. Like a medicine which was labelled, 'good until 1968'. If used in 1972, the medicine is entirely ineffective. The body is the bottle, the karma in the body is the medicine. God puts a date on the 'medicine' so it is not effective.

H: But Swami, grace is a rare prescription!

Sai: It might be thought that grace is difficult to secure. Such is not the case. Grace is the easiest thing to secure if the method is known and used. In the Gita, the method is given. As in driving a car, so confusing at first, but with practice it is so easy to do all the necessary tasks all at the same time and also carry on a conversation without strain. There is nothing that cannot be accomplished with practice. Even ants in a single file crossing a stone will leave a mark. The Name; it is that which will guard you and guide you throughout life. It is such a small thing! But to cross the ocean, an immense steamship is not needed. Even a small raft will do. The Name of God is the smallest of the small, and the largest of the large. The mouth is the principal gateway of the body, and the tongue must always carry the Name. Like a small lantern, the Name must go when and where you go, and then you can travel easily through the whole forest of life.

XLII

H: Baba's dramatic recovery from what the doctors considered as sure death, during the Goa incident, must have amazed and puzzled the doctors?

Sai: The next morning, after Baba had at 4 p.m. walked down the 150 steps from the palace to the platform from which he delivered a spiritual discourse, there was a conference of the 25 doctors who had been called by the Governor to consult over Baba, along with quite a number of their medical students. The argument was, how could a body with a ruptured appendix and without an operation continue to live? The top doctor said, 'We are in a useless discussion, Sri Sathya Sai is divine.' Baba created 25 rings all at once, one for each doctor. They have now all surrendered to Baba, and they call 'Sai Ram' before treating any patient. The radio reported Baba as dying. The best doctors in India were called in. Baba was black in colour. The doctors gave him varying times of up to a maximum of ten minutes or so to live. Baba then declared that he would lecture in the afternoon, that he had taken on the illness of a devotee. India's most prominant doctor said, 'That may be so, but I say you are about to die'. Baba said, 'See at 4 p.m.'.

H: Is it true that Swami suffered some extreme abuse from doctors when He was a boy?

Sai: Baba underwent torture at the hands of the village doctors when he first allowed His divine powers to manifest on a fairly large scale. This was around the age of 10. The doctors drilled holes in His head and stuck in hot irons, cut open His skin and poured in burning fluids, buried Him in a trench with sand up to His neck and iron bars to keep Him fixed in position. Here, He would just move and be free despite the iron bars. During all the torture, He smiled and felt no pain. He at no time had even the slightest body identification. When Baba was born, He knew His Divinity and that he was God Himself. The universe is held in Baba's hand and He could, in an instant, make the entire universe vanish.

H: Swami, please say some things about Your early childhood?

Sai: Swami had two shirts and pants to last a year. There was no money even for a pin. Thorns were used to hold torn places together. Tears in the cloth came from schoolmates who would punish Baba for always knowing the answers at school. Only He would know the answer. If He gave the answer the boys would beat Him. If He did not give it, the teacher would beat Him. On some occasions, the pupil who answered had to slap the faces of those who did not. Since Swami was small, He had to stand on a chair to slap, But He would slap gently. Then the teacher would slap Him hard as many times as He had slapped gently. Of course, after the immediate retaliation of the boys, they would be loving and affectionate to Baba. Even though Baba had not even a pin for Himself, He would produce pens, pencils, notebook paper, or whatever the boys needed. This, at length, led to some fear in the village. Because, how could it be explained to the authorities as to how these things were present? At one stage, after the age of 11, Baba was kept more or less out of circulation for a couple of years. At that time the liberation of India was in process. The police were moving in the villages and arresting Congress members, and so on.

H: The early stories are extraordinary! They do not conform to anything that we could imagine. Those childhood companions, they must have been quite special. Was their further destiny unusual also?

Sai: Concerning the seat in school, there were two boys who sat with Swami in the same seat. It was for three. When Swami declared that He would no longer go to school, one boy committed suicide. The other boy went mad. He would call, 'Raju Raju' all the time. At length he died.

H: It is very strange; a great mystery. But was his death a good death because his mind was fixed on Swami and constantly calling Swami's name?

Sai: He merged with me. There was also a Telugu teacher who took pains to get himself appointed to Swami's school, and who left the school as soon as Swami left.

XLIII

A Visitor: Is an exercise program important? In the West, exercise is considered to be of great value.

Sai: Exercise is extolled in the West as a way to digest excess food and sublimate the sex drive. Swami, who is completely removed from the area of sensory thoughts, takes a very small quantity of food, and needs no exercise. Yet his body is very strong. For those engaged in work, that is exercise. The idea of exercise comes to those who are idle and who do not have the full responsibility of work. Moderation in life is necessary, otherwise there is no reserve of energy. Food must be in the body for some time for the benefit of the energy reserve. Too much exercise uses up the food energy before it can be added to the reserve. So there is no gain. Likewise, the human system cannot withstand too much talking. One M. P. talked for two hours and felt dizzy. Nobody can continue talking—that is, nobody except Swami who has been doing it for years and years.

XLIV

H: Swami, hippies are seen wherever one goes. It is difficult for an older person to relate to that sub-culture. It does not seem to express values that can be taken seriously.

Sai: The hippies' ideas are based on no work, drugs, begging, free relationship between the sexes. Baba gave some of them work to do in the print shop. They did not do it. Baba offered funds to go home, they did not want to go. They do not understand 'karma,' that work produces results, as such is understood in India. Dharma does not have an equivalent word in English. Righteousness is work. Truth in words, and truth and love in the heart is dharma.

H: How does one determine the particular dharma appropriate to himself?

Sai: One has to enquire. Ask questions such as, 'I am a man, what is animal work? Am I male or female? Am I young or old? And so forth. Because animal behavior is not correct for humans. And a man should not behave like a woman. If an old person plays with dolls, like a child, he is ridiculous. If a youngster takes a cane and walks like an old person, he is ridiculous. That work which is righteous, true, well considered in truth, is dharma. Thought, word and deed must coincide. The other person must be understood. You feel hunger if another person is hungry. You must feel his hunger as your own.

H: When does one really experience that he is the same as another? Now, one feels for another through compassion. But compassion is not direct experience. When someone hit a dog, Shirdi Sai Baba had the bruises. That is the actual experience of unity.

Sai: All is divine. When you are firmly established in the fact of your divinity, then you will directly know that others

115

are divine. Compassion for others is felt as long as you consider yourself as a separate entity. The story about Shirdi Sai Baba as related in books is not fully correct. The facts are that a lady made a plate of sweets for Shirdi Baba, and a dog ate them. The lady drove the dog away with blows. She then carried another platter of sweets to Shirdi Baba, who refused them, saying that He had eaten the sweets she previously provided and His hunger was satisfied. The lady objected that this was the first time the sweets had been offered, so how could Baba say to the contrary? Baba said, 'No,' that she had offered them before and had also beaten Him. In this way, He gave a lesson that He was omnipresent and that there was only one life. During the lifetime of Shirdi Baba not much attention was paid to Him. Recognition of Him as an Avatar, and interest in His life developed only after His 'death'. Thus, various incidents are called from memory now by devotees and written down in books. The same lack of recognition of divinity is illustrated in the lives of Rama and Krishna. Krishna was considered as just a cow-herd boy, and then as just a charioteer. Even the life of Shirdi Baba prior to age 18 is known only to Baba, and the divinity was known only to a very few genuine devotees.

H: It seems strange that only a few people recognize the Avatar.

Sai: No, not strange. How would you know the Avatar?

H: By faith.

Sai: Faith is one thing. Knowing is another. Your wife may have faith in you, but she does not know you. The Avatar may be known at one time, but doubt arises and recognition wavers. An example is Viswamitra, the great sage, who asked for the company of the young lads Rama and Lakshmana, to help him overcome the demons who were disrupting his performance of Vedic ceremonies. He said to the king that he did not want the king's powerful armies, that the two boys, who were divine incarnations, were sufficient. Yet, upon reaching their destination, he called Rama in order to instruct him in mantras that would overcome the demons. Waves of maya make recognition of the Avatar almost impossible.

H: But Swami, that is still very strange. Recognition of the Avatar was so difficult in those ancient, simpler days, yet in this corrupt and complicated society, recognition of the Avatar is almost world-wide.

Sai: Is it widespread? There are stories and articles about Swami, but how many persons are sure that he is the Avatar, and how many of those who are sure are free of doubt? Another example: you know Swami as the Avatar?

H: Yes.

Sai: No doubts?

H: No doubts whatsoever.

Sai: Your own experience is that Swami is omnipresent?

H: Yes, that is my direct experience.

Sai: Yet, when you leave Swami at Brindavan and arrive at your hotel you think of Swami as being at Brindavan. You see, it is not so easy to know the omnipresent Avatar. Of course, there are always some who know. In the Krishna Avatara, there were some who knew. Likewise, there were some who knew the Rama Avatara. Not every blossom opens to the sun when it rises. Only some are ready. There is the factor of ripeness. Not every fruit on a tree is ripe at the same time. Another example: who offers that new house, and to whom is it given?

H: To the divine form.

Sai: What? Divine form? This is the divine form? This is a human body. When the name of Swami is placed on a transfer of deed, to whom is the deed transferred, and who makes the transfer? Is it not from that body to this body?

H: Yes, from body to body.

Sai: Exactly. (The implication being that if Swami were really recognized as the Avatar, both the offer and the question of acceptance would be without meaning, and neither would occur.)

H: Sometimes Swami speaks of the Ramayana and the

Mahabharata as if they were historical, and sometimes as if they were to be taken as representative of every individual's inner conflicts, virtues, bad qualities, etc. Are these events and people historical fact?

Sai: Yes, they are a record of historical people and incidents. But in themselves, the battles and troubles of these families are unimportant. What is of lasting significance is the inner spiritual significance of the happening. Rama was a real person and an Avatar. And Dasaratha was His father. Krishna was real and the events of His Avatara were real. Rama's life, over the ages, has been altered and distorted somewhat, and Swami's story of Rama will be a classic through several Yugas. In the time of Krishna, the viewpoint was different, and actions occurred that would be viewed in a different light today.

H: Swami once mentioned that if we could see Rama today we would be much surprised at His appearance.

Sai: Every age has its own circumstances, traditions and values, so it should not surprise us if everyone is not just like ourselves. Even today there are such differences. In African forests, people have their own ideas of what is beauty. For example, they distort lips, nostrils and ears. In the age prior to that of Rama, people were accustomed to take as their unit of measure the distance from the finger tips to the elbow. At that time, the norm for the height of a person was 14 times that measurement. Thus, the height of every person would have its own harmony. In the Threta Yuga, the age of Rama, the norm for height had reduced to seven times the distance of finger-tip to elbow. For the Kali Yuga, the multiple is three and one-half. The description of Rama is, 'That which charms.' Extraordinary divine charm was a particular characteristic of Rama's person. His features were perfect and had a beauty that pulled the heart of every person who saw Him. His figure was likewise perfect. Height and limbs were in perfect symmetry.

H: We read that even the demons were unable to resist the charm of Rama.

Sai: The Yakshas were called demons, but even they

prostrated before Rama when they perceived His charming face and figure. The Yakshas had deformed faces. Sometimes the nose was missing. Sometimes the eyes were very deeply set.

H: What about Krishna? How would He be described?

Sai: The situation was somewhat different with Krishna. He had the quality of attraction. All were attracted to him and wished to come very close to him.

H: Krishna was quite young then, was He not?

Sai: Krishna was always young. In years, he was six or seven. The Gopis would pet Him like a child.

H: In those days they had airplanes, did they not?

Sai: The first was 'Pushpak', the one Ravana used to kidnap Sita. Indian Airlines is now building a small plane by the same name.

H: Did they use atomic energy for power?

Sai: No. By the power of a mantra the plane would fly. Mantras were also used to shoot arrows. The arrows were worshipped to make them effective. When Arjuna heard of Krishna's death, he forgot all mantras and was powerless. Today, at the festival of Navarathri, the farmers worship their farm implements with mantra and that has an effect.

H: Then even today, mantras still have effect?

Sai: Oh, yes. Even Westerners who experiment with the Gayatri mantra find it has power. The mantra should be said by a person well practiced in spiritual life.

H: Swami does not seem to give out mantras. When His devotees are ready for mantra should they ask Swami, or will He say when they are ready?

Sai: Mantras now are given out by low persons, the head of a Mutt here and there, some yogi, and so on. Avatars have never given mantras. The Avatar shows that God is everywhere. The recitation of a mantra is narrow minded. In the time of an Avatar, to hear him, to understand what he says and to do it is a mantra. Krishna gave no mantra to the Pandava brothers, not even to Arjuna. He simply said, 'Do this. . .do that.' This was enough, and the action was very powerful.

H: Baba's teaching carries the ring of truth, and His words carry into action almost by themselves. Their authority does not even depend on whether Swami is an Avatar or not.

Sai: Don't doubt about the Avatar as Swami. Without His reading it, any question asked Baba is answered immediately, without any pause, and in detail.

H: An incident of Sri Krishna's life that I do not understand is that when He instructed Arjuna to conduct the women and children to safety, Arjuna failed. Why?

Sai: Arjuna always felt that Krishna was in his heart, and that gave him his strength. When he heard that Krishna had died, he felt that Krishna was gone and, as he felt this, his strength left him.

H: But Swami, if Arjuna had Krishna in his heart, why did Krishna's death have such an effect?

Sai: For some 80 years Arjuna felt Krishna was with him in his heart. The reaction of shock at the news of Krishna's death caused him to momentarily forget. It was weakness. Then, he was not able to recapture the feeling of Krishna being with him.

H: If Arjuna had kept the feeling and concept of Krishna in his heart, would he have retained his strength?

Sai: When he heard that Krishna had died, he lost all interest in the world.

H: The Gopis were overcome with grief when Krishna departed from there. They must have had Him in their hearts.

Sai: At the news of Krishna's death, a number of the Gopis fell lifeless from shock.

H: Then their relationship was only with the form of Krishna?

Sai: The Gopis had both relationships. Because of their years of close companionship with Krishna, they were strongly attached to Krishna's physical presence. But they also knew Krishna in their hearts. They always felt He was with them, even when His worldly activity had taken Him far away.

H: Then why the terrible shock, if Krishna was so firmly known in the heart?

Sai: The Gopis had no interest in the world and the body once Krishna was dead. Their only reason for placing any value on their physical existence was because Krishna was also in physical existence. Their hearts were completely pure, and Krishna was their heart. The physical bond was also strong. For example, you have proof that Swami is always with you, but at the same time, you wish to come to India to be near Swami, isn't it?

H: Seems to me that this episode of Arjuna and the death of Krishna carries a very important lesson for us who live today.

Sai: There is no need to take Arjuna as a model. Just realize that God is with you and in your heart at all times.

H: Might an Avatar be born in some other part of the world?

Sai: Buddha, Christ, Mohammed and others were not Avatars. They had some divine power. Only in India are Avatars born, because only in India are the Sastras understood; and only in India do the sages constantly experiment and practice. It is like in a gold mine. Where gold is found, there gather the geologists, engineers, and experienced miners. The gold is mined there, and then it is taken all over the world.

XLV

H: Some persons visit a number of ashrams, and there is certainly a temptation to do this.

Sai: In America, there is so much restlessness that people grasp anything purported to be spiritual in order to find a little peace. But that peace is temporary. Spiritual organizations may have some value at the beginning level. They encourage the person to start enquiring for God. Enquiry is 3/4 and sadhana 1/4. One has the right to enquire about a saint. How does he act, why is it thus, and thus. But going to many gurus is like a man who owns an acre. He digs a bit here, then moves over to

121

a new spot and digs a little, and so on. Finally, he digs one hole five feet deep and finds water. The total of all his diggings was perhpas 30 feet. At last, in one digging, he did find water, but his acre was spoiled by the many shallow holes dug here and there. Had he stayed with one hole and dug 30 feet, he would have had his water. The acre is the spiritual heart. All the holes are different gurus. Now the spiritual heart is ruined by so many holes; they are leaks.

A Visitor: What is a guru?

Sai: A guru is a light to show one the road, but the destination is God. One is grateful to the guru, but it is God that one worships. Nowadays, one worships the guru, which is quite wrong.

H: Suppose that guru is the Lord Himself. How would that change the picture?

Sai: (laughs) It changes the picture a great deal. If the Lord is one's guru, no need to worry about anything. Just as a loving mother cares for her child, if one has surrendered his life to God with full faith in Him, the Lord takes care of that devotee. No need to worry about anything. Really, guru is only God. God is within only. Those outside are not gurus. They are teachers of one sort or another. Guru means, 'He who removes darkness'. Only God can remove the darkness within; only by God's grace.

H: In this business of sadhana, why is it not possible from the very start to take the Lord as guru and surrender one's life to Him?

Sai: (again laughing) That is not so easy! It is very difficult to do. First one needs to tame the mind. It is just like a wild elephant in the forest. It must be caught and tamed. Once subdued and tamed, it is like an elephant in a circus who can be made to sit on a small stool by a small boy. And that is the result of training and practice.

A Visitor: The problem of training the mind seems very difficult. Why not take the path of love?

Sai: Love also is not that easy. In the world there can be too much love, which leads to unbalanced action. Indian culture manages wives by keeping them fully occupied in the house. But for the divine, love may be unlimited; there is no danger. 'Worldly' love should have a limit. But love of God is unbounded; it has no limit. Lack of understanding is not too dangerous, but misunderstanding is very dangerous. In America, the movies, although bad, are taken for granted. In India, they corrupt and destroy respect for womanhood.

A Visitor: How about American gurus?

Sai: People come from America, learn some yoga, return to America, put up a board, 'Yoga Institute,' and become leaders. They read a few books, then offer to answer all questions. The real leader practices and lives his philosophy, and then people look to him because they see life in what he says.

H: How should we regard these many gurus here and there in the world? Some of them seem to do much good, but Swami has no good word for them. They talk very well about the divine, and they collect many disciples.

Sai: The proper course is for that person to admit that he does not know God, and to suggest that he and his followers jointly investigate, and practice sadhana. But they do not do that. The idea is to pick up an answer here and an answer there, then give out the information like a phonograph recording, pretending it is their own wisdom. One such person has a son over whom he has no authority or influence. A man cannot guide his own family, but sets himself up as a guide for others. It is ridiculous.

H: Another type of guru is the Indian who comes to America. The outstanding example is a man who is known internationally and whose followers may even run into the millions. Through him people become interested in India, learn meditation, and there are thousands of reports of the beneficial effects on the lives of the followers. Is not a guru such as this of some value?

Sai: A million people sit cross-legged in meditation. Not one gains liberation from bondage. What is the point of it all? If even the guru gained liberation, there might be some value. But even that does not happen. And if some slight mistake is made, there is great harm. The net effect of it all is that it spoils both guru and disciple. The apparent benefit is only temporary; it is not permanent. You have had considerable genuine experience. Will you be a guru?

H: God forbid! On no account would I be a guru. I cannot imagine anything I would be more against. I'm even against the appearance of it!

Sai: That is it! That is the right path. That way you are a guru. The genuine guru never sets himself up as a guru. He proceeds with his own sadhana, keeping out of public notice. By observing his life, one or two people will pursue him and force him to disclose or share something of value, and such aspirants may get some genuine help from such a person.

XLVI

Sai: (at the start of an interview with a group of westerners) Follow the master, the inside Atma, the super-conscious. Life is a challenge; fight to the end. Life is a song; sing it. Life is divine; realize it. Life is character. There is one path, complete life.

Sai: (to a young westerner, about age 16) What do you want?

Boy: Liberation.

Sai: What is liberation?

Boy: (after some hesitation) The end of the path.

Sai: Immortality is the meaning. Removal of immorality is the only way to immortality. Who are you? Not the outside, not the body. Who are you? Enquire. Love is everything. Expansion love, not selfish love. Selfless love of the Self; not ego love. All are ladies. None are men. Lady is weakness, not strength. The Sanskrit word for lady has the meaning of

124

weakness; no strength at all. All humans are so. Hate, anger, jealousy, sorrow. Men may better control these, but their inside feeling is the same. Only God is above feeling. All others are equally affected. God is the only male person. In a women's college, in a play, men characters may appear on the stage, but the male cast are women dressed as men. The world is a women's college. There are just male roles. Inside all are the same, all women. Life is a cosmic stage on which we are the actors. In one scene an actor may take one role, and in other scenes different roles. Creation means change. Nothing is unchanging. Every moment there is change. How can these changing things give bliss to persons who are also changing? Your bliss can be made permanent only by immortality, no change. Scientists experiment today; tomorrow their findings are outmoded. The world goes on overriding itself. That which science knows is microscopic compared to the immensity of that which is to be known. The atom: Without this, nothing is made. With atoms all things are produced. Atoms together also make the moon. Atoms are active and alert, never inert. How therefore, can the moon be called inert? The entire universe is active because of atoms. From where does this energy come? Electrons, neutrons, protons—from where does this science arise? Scientists ask how is it that these things go on, but do not ask, 'Why?' The answer to 'why' leads you to the divine. Basic energy is shakthi. From this basic energy all is derived. Wherefrom this atom power? It is divine power.

Hislop asked the question, 'What is a study circle?' It is not just reading books. 'Circle, study circle' means taking a point and each person discussing what is the meaning of the point to them. Like a round-table conference. Each person gives his point of view, and finally values are derived from this. If there is just reading, there is doubt. But if each one gives his view, doubts will be answered. The topic is viewed; the study circle looks at different facets. It is like a diamond with its different facets, but there is one facet that is flat, the top facet, and from this all can be viewed. To discover the top facet is the task of

125

the study circle. Swami's talks may be taken, or other scriptures. Take a point. Have everyone think about it and discuss it, and come to the final point where doubt is decreased. If only one person reads, there will be only one meaning. All misunderstandings, all points of views—after these are brought out, the study circle members will get confidence. There is no doubt of this. If each one only reads, this may go on for a year or two, then an allergy to reading develops. Centers must have study circles in this way, and none will note the passage of time. Each one listens eagerly and many will give their point of view. The Bible, the Koran, the Gita, Swami's books may be used. What is wanted is a study circle; rotating. Each one must be given a chance.

A Scientist Visitor: (father of the 16-year-old boy earlier questioned by Swami) Many fools do not make one wise man.

Sai: Only those who are intelligent will think to bother with a study circle. They may be fools in other matters, perhaps. But we have here the example of a big doctor who does operations but who in bandaging is a fool, reliant upon his nurse to do a good job. Life means such a mixture. A man with a dual mind is half blind. Everyone is half blind in some matters. Only he who knows the divine is an expert, first class in one study. But in general, people have no common sense. But common sense is necessary in daily life, and that is what counts. Each subject is only one road; but mastery, the development of common sense is a spiritual effort. In a house an elder is not respected, because Junior studied some subjects, but common sense requires that Junior's attitude to the elder be respectful. Common sense is required. Humility and love are divine. If you become the master of a subject, and develop anger and ego, these are enemies of the spiritual path.

Scientist: But it is commonly agreed that science is of great value.

Sai: Up to a certain level, science helps. It is of service to mankind. But Baba knows that which science does not know. Baba is at a level that is beyond reach of the senses. Not all

126

that he knows can be brought to a lower level. Too much current burns out the bulb. Capacities must be known. Swami's power is given according to capacity. Baba is the servant. He waits at the door of the shrine room to give you what you want. To be the servant of his devotees is Swami's duty. There is no place for any ego. A small example: On a globe-map of the world, America is not very big. California is just a small place. Hislop's house is just a dot; and Hislop himself is not even visible. For a person, so small as to be invisible, so temporary in the expanse of the universe, to live with ego is shameful. Any person with ego is a disgrace. If you expand your idea of yourself to be God, then there is no reason, no place for an ego. And if you shrink yourself to conform to your relative stature in the vast universe, there is also no place for ego. The lowest or the highest, it does not matter. It is the middle that has pressure.

H: From Swami's description of the conversation to be accomplished in a study circle, the circle should be limited to about 10 people.

Sai: Why? It could be 100 people.

H: But Swami, not even one point would be able to get around such a big circle.

Sai: Not so. Of the group here, only the scientist and Hislop are asking questions. Not everyone in the study circle will be able to say.

H: Oh. I see that situation.

Scientist: Here is this object. I spoke about Swami in Copenhagen, and some scientists who were interested made this object. What it is cannot be seen. The scientists know, but it cannot be seen.

Sai: It is Baba's task to transform peoples' hearts.

H: They are trying to subject Baba to a test! (the scientist and his associate had for several years past been trying to get Swami to subject Himself to wires and electronic measurements and so on).

Sai: Baba can transform the scientists, but scientists can

transform themselves only by getting into the spiritual life. It is only physics in which they are engaged. Philosophy starts where physics ends. Physics is useful, but it is only information. Spiritual life is transformation.

Scientist: Baba does miracles to shake up disbelievers.

Sai: Baba does it for His own sake. Let the scientists come, and I will transform them. The spiritual world is beyond the material. Material things are involved in sorrow. Have great scientists compassion and a peaceful mind? No. They worry and worry. What is needed is to unite spiritual life and worldly life. Spiritual life is developed first, and then live a spiritual life in the world, a dual life. Spiritual life is quality, and worldly life is quantity.

Scientist: It is of value to let scientists test you.

Sai: What is the value?

Scientist: If they can be convinced that the miracles are valid by scientific controls and standards, then belief in you will follow.

Sai: If they believe, what will the world gain? Their worldly desires will increase since their understanding is so poor.

Scientist: It takes time. Science consolidates its gains only gradually.

Sai: Even they do not understand their own science fully enough. It is good that they go slowly.

XLVII

A Visitor: Is it not better to have a qualified nursemaid to care for a child when the mother is nervous and unable to give proper attention?

Sai: The nursemaid gives love that is purchased. The mother's love is real. Give a child to servants and the child's thoughts are cultured at the servant's level.

A Visitor: Swami, the cement floor in my room is very hard.

128

Sai: Baba instructs by life in the Ashram. Up early and to bed early so that the mind is bright and alert. Live on the floor to learn that the body has few genuine needs.

XLVIII

(Hislop and an interpreter were having breakfast with Swami. Two men, Mr. XY and Mr. CD, entered the room, and Mr. XY fell at Swami's feet. He was in tears, and it was obvious that some grave and sad errand had brought him to Swami. Hislop and his companion immediately left the room. Shortly, after the two men left, Baba called Hislop and his companion into his presence again. Names of persons have been changed so as not to discuss identities.)

Sai: When Sai's mother died, the summer course was on. Sai sent the body to Puttaparthi, but did not accompany it. His duty was the summer course. The case of Sri XY will illustrate how Swami takes care of His devotees. At the XY house, there were only the women and the body of Mrs. XY. Nobody to take care. Not even a priest to chant the required Vedic hymns. Swami drove directly from Prasanthi Nilayam to the XY house taking a Vedic priest from the ashram in the car with Him. Swami comforted the women and made all the needed arrangements before driving on to Brindavan. Then He sent a senior man from the Brindavan household to the house so that the ladies would not be alone in the house overnight. Sai is the close and the real relative of His devotees. The ladies of the XY household left their sorrow and all became happy with Sai's shower of grace.

H: Swami was not told, but somehow He must have known when the lady died?

Sai: Swami knew well before the time of her death. He made all the necessary arrangements at that time, even sending a special message to Hislop on Tuesday the 16th that the college celebration would not be held on the 25th, but not to tell the students. Mrs. XY was born on a full moon day and she died on a full moon day.

H: Why did she die? Was it that her time to die had arrived?

Sai: Her time to die arrived several years ago. But she prayed to Swami that before she died she wanted to see her grandson married, and she wanted to witness the celebration of Swami's birthday. Swami granted her prayer. She also had a third desire, although she did not mention it. She had the desire that prior to her death she would spend some days with her youngest son. When she was at Prasanthi Nilayam in November, she said to Swami that her grandson had married and that she was now witnessing Swami's birthday celebration and that she was now content to die anytime. Her major desires in life had all been fulfilled. Swami replied that if she died now, her husband, who was abroad, would not be here. She said that Swami was here and that she was holding to Him and to nobody else. Swami told her that she should go to the city of her youngest son and visit with him for some days, and she did so. On Dec. 18 she was to return to her own home because her husband would arrive home from his trip abroad on Dec. 19. On the 18th, her son was driving her to the airport and she was talking to him from the back seat of the car. Then, there was no further talk from her. She became silent. The son turned to look and saw her fallen on her side. She was gone.

H: Without any pain?

Sai: No pain, no suffering. She was in good health and was gone in an instant. The son turned the car and returned home. Had the mother died at the airport, the body would have been impounded. The son turned the car around on the highway and immediately drove home. When he got to his house there was a phone call from Baba waiting for him. Baba had instructed one of the ashram officials to place the phone call with the message to 'send the body at once to your father's house.' The ashram official was puzzled at the message, since he knew nothing about 'a body.' Swami then phoned Mr. CD, the man who just now brought Mr. XY to Swami, and had him fly to Bombay to meet Mr. XY at the airport and bring him to Brindavan. That was the occasion that you just now witnessed. Mr. CD was not to tell XY about the death of his wife until such time as they were just about to arrive here. When you saw XY, he was overcome by the sudden news. The sequence of events was perfectly harmonized. When devotees surrender their lives to God and obey Him, He takes the full responsibility and cares for His devotees even to the smallest details. One last point. When Swami reached the XY home after driving there from Prasanthi Nilayam, he arranged that the body be properly prepared and would remain so until XY drove home after seeing Baba and being comforted by him. Thus, by harmoniously relating all details, Swami even allowed XY to see the features of his wife and take the correct farewell.

H: Swami! Here, just now, we actually witnessed a part of this amazing story. How can all that be? Swami holds the entire universe in His Hand. He bears the responsibility for the inconceivable, immense universe. And how can He at the same time give this detailed attention to the lives of individual devotees?

Sai: It is as you say. Swami holds the universe in His Hand. But devotees learn of the glory and majesty through Swami's attention to each one, personally. That Swami holds the universe yet at the same time fully cares for the lives of His devotees even to the smallest details is a measure of His glory that the devotee can understand.

H: Swami! How is it that Swami makes a perfect harmony in one case, as with the death of Mrs. XY, and yet in another case, that of which we were speaking just before XY arrived, there is anything but harmony; indeed, there is a highly imperfect situation. This is a big puzzle.

Sai: It depends on the people involved. In the case of a devotee who has pure thoughts and a pure heart and who has surrendered to Bhagavan, then Swami takes full responsibility for that life and takes care of that devotee. But where a person has a big ego, relying on ego desire and not on Bhagavan, then Swami keeps a distance and does not interfere.

H: Oh. I see the difference.

Sai: Swami could make the situation perfect in regards to that individual. But where there is a big ego and the person wishes to follow ego desire, Swami does not interfere, but allows the person to do as he wishes.

H: Swami says to cut to the very roots of desire. What does "cutting the roots" mean?

Sai: If desire comes, analyze it. If it is good for you and not harmful to others, go ahead. If not good, put it aside at once. If you are uncertain, do nothing until the uncertainty is clarified.

H: Is it wrong to critize a person?

Sai: It is not wrong to criticize a person if the evaluation has been arrived at slowly and carefully.

XLIX

A Visitor: How to get enough faith for even meditation? There is no time.

Sai: Not true. We always have enough time to talk, visit, cinema, etc. There is certainly time for meditation.

A Visitor: After meditation there is a feeling of strength. Where does that power come from and what is its relation to meditation?

Sai: The power is from God. The relationship between God and the devotee is love. It is almost impossible to be aware of the relationship with God. God is the subtlest of the subtle, and the relationship with Him is of the same subtlety.

A Visitor: Swami said that meditation twice a day is best?

Sai: Early morning is best. Mind is quiet and there is not the pressure of responsibilities.

H: Is meditation from time to time during the day all right?

Sai: There is difficulty during the day. People are around, and there is work. If meditation is attempted, even work may suffer.

A Visitor: What is meditation?

Sai: Real meditation is getting absorbed in God as the only thought, the only goal. God only, only God. Think God, breathe God, love God, live God.

Visitor: What about concentration?

Sai: Concentration means, when all senses and desires fall away and there is only God. The concentration of Ramakrishna Paramahaṃsa was naturally so strong that he grew something of a tail when meditating on Hanuman, the monkey. His body was just a changing bubble, his concentration was so strong. Special work on concentration need not be a part of meditation. Concentration is already in force wherever mind, intelligence and senses are used. Without it you could not even walk. It needs no special practice. It is below the senses. Meditation is above the senses. In between concentration and meditation, like a separation between the two, is contemplation. Concentration to contemplation, then meditation. As long as one thinks, 'I am meditating'; that is the mind and is not meditation. As long as one knows he is meditating, he is not meditating. In that absorption in God, one puts aside every form and merges into God. In that process the mind naturally stops.

A Visitor: Baba says to cut off form in meditation, but we worship Swami's form.

Sai: That is all right to do. But when one comes close to Baba, the visualization is abandoned. At this moment, you are looking at Baba directly. Are you still visualizing?

A Visitor: What should I do? My meditation is the enquiry, 'Who am I?'

Sai: The Ramana Maharshi enquiry by itself is not good. It must be combined with meditation. Meditation, for its proper practice, should be at the same place, at the same time. In that way, it surely will be successful. If one is away from home in travel, in his mind he can go to the accustomed place no matter where he is. To search for truth is needless. Truth is every place at all times. One must live truth, not search for it. 'Kohum' (Who am I) is the cry of the newborn child. After a lifetime of Sadhana, the old man says, 'Sohum' (I am God). When away from Swami, by remembering Him doing this or that, the battery is 'recharged.' That also is genuine meditation. Meditation is constant inner enquiry as to who am I, what is true, what is ego action, what is loving and what is harsh. Meditation is thinking on spiritual principles, searching out the application to oneself of what Baba says, and the like.

H: Mr. 'X' does kriya yoga.

Sai: He does bad kriya.

H: He does much meditation and practices kundalini yoga.

Sai: Kundalini shakthi is balance in mind and action.

H: But Swami, kundalini yoga is supposed to mean the kundalini power rising up the spine.

Sai: That is not real. It is just speeches. People claim this happening and boast about it. It is big ego.

H: Does Swami mean that in fact there is no kundalini power or energy that starts at the base of the spine and rises up the spine?

Sai: There is no such thing. That is just big talk and big ego. Yogi 'S' (a yoga teacher) is full of greed, ego, hate.

H: Swami praises pranayama and pratyahara.

Sai: First there is control of outer senses, then control of inner senses, then a sense of balance with a limitation to freedom; because freedom is the end of wisdom. Then comes pranayama and pratyahara.

H: But Swami praises the two. In which way should devotees act on that?

Sai: All of these, like hatha yoga and so on, are like exams. You study and pass the exam and then you feel confident and proud. It is like going to college. There are eight principal stages and you work and reach each one. But they are necessary only if you go to college. For the one who has completely surrendered to God and whose heart is filled with love for God, these 'college courses' are not needed and have no meaning. They are quite unnecessary.

H: Does the Atma have a location in the body where the

attention may be fixed in meditation? Is the Atma considered to have a 'seat'?

Sai: The Atma is everywhere, but for the purpose of sitting in meditation, the life principle can be considered as being 10 'inches' above the navel and at the centre of the chest. An 'inch' in this measurement is the width of the thumb at the first joint.

H: I have read that the seat of the Atma is found to be at the right side of chest centre, that is where one points at himself.

Sai: That the seat of the Self is at the right is just a viewpoint. Left handed people point differently.

H: Once the individual is absorbed in meditation, there is the question of how long to sit.

Sai: There is no answer. There is no particular time. Meditation is really an all day long process.

H: Swami points out that we already have and use a very high order of concentration in our daily lives. Then why is concentration not automatic in spiritual practice?

Sai: Without concentration nothing can be done. And we use that concentration throughout the day. Why is that same concentration so difficult to come by in spiritual matters? Because the mind is outward turned, and by desire the mind clings to objects. But the mind can be trained to concentrate inwardly, and the heart can be cultured to grow with love for God. How? By sadhana. The best sadhana is that every act through the day be done as worship of God. God is like electric power. The heart is the light bulb. The wiring is the discipline. The switch is the intelligence. The act of turning the switch is morning, noon or evening meditation. Once the electric switch, the wiring and bulb are in, nothing more need be done. Just turn the switch and there is light. A fence is placed around a young tree to protect it. The same precautions must be observed in meditation. People think it is all right to meditate any place. There are currents, there is will power. There is a strong current passing into the earth. Because of this, the earth exerts a very strong attraction. In meditation it is advisable to insulate oneself from such current. For this reason, meditators sit on a plank and cover their shoulders with a woolen shawl. Once the person has grown strong in his meditation, he may sit anywhere and not suffer for it.

H: There must be a second or a fraction between one thought and another, and also between sleep and waking. No doubt that state between must be something special?

Sai: Find out. Continue practice to catch the intervals between sleep and waking. Do it with love.

H: Swami, seeing a corpse one can understand that the body has no life of its own. But how can the mind be associated with a body that is inert?

Sai: There is the inert body. There is the supreme consciousness. And in between the two there is the mind which also is inert but which appears to be alive because it is infused with consciousness. Just as with iron which when heated burns and does so because it has been penetrated by fire; thus it is not the iron that burns, but it is the fire that burns. The whole mirage, the whole thing arises from thought. From the identification of 'I' with the body, all troubles and complications arise. Since it is the mind that has woven this web of identification with the body, it is the mind that must now turn and seek one's true nature through discrimination, renunciation and enquiry. Both ego and intelligence may be included in the word, 'mind.'

H: Swami, in meditation some of the westerners are taking light alone, not the quite definite form of the jyoti, but just a formless light and they are concentrating on that and projecting that. Is it correct to take formless light as the object of concentration?

Sai: It is not practical to attempt to concentrate on that which has no form. To concentrate on the jyoti, is an illustration. The object of concentration can be sound, form, the jyoti, etc. It needs to be something concrete. It is not easy to fix the mind on the abstract.

H: Is there a particular pathway along which the flame, the jyoti, should be moved in the body?

Sai: The light is first moved into the heart which is conceived as a lotus, the petals of which will open. The jyoti is then moved to other body parts. There is no particular sequence. But important is the final body station, which is the head. There the light becomes a crown enshrining and covering the head. The light is then moved outside, from the particular to the universal. Move the light into relatives, friends, enemies, trees, animals, birds until the entire world and all its forms are seen to have the same light at their centre as has been found to be within oneself. The idea of moving the light into the universal phase, the idea of universality is that the same divine light is present in everyone and everywhere. To impress this universality on the mind, we do the spreading of the light outside one's own body. One should understand that what comes about in meditation as one moves deeply into it, is not the thinking of the light, but the forgetting of the body and thereby the direct experience that the body is not oneself. This is the stage of contemplation when the body is totally forgotten. It cannot be forced. It comes about by itself and is the stage that naturally follows correct concentration. Vivekananda told that in meditation he was unable to find his body; where was his body? He could not find it. Seeing the light and moving the light here and there is to give work to the mind, to keep the mind occupied in the right direction so that the mind will not be thinking of this and that and thus interfering with the process of becoming more and more quiet. Spreading the light into its universal phase, sending the light into every other body, when one is so concentrated in that he is not longer conscious of his body, is the stage of contemplation. As contemplation deepens, the stage of meditation comes about of its own volition. It cannot be forced. If the meditator remains conscious of himself and that he is engaged in meditation, then he is not meditating but is still in the preliminary stage, at the beginning of concentration. There are the three stages: concentration, contemplation and meditation. When contemplation deepens it moves naturally into meditation. Meditation is entirely above the senses. In the state of meditation the meditator, the object of his meditation and the process of meditation have fallen away, and there is only one, and that One is God. All that may change has fallen away and Tat Twam Asi, That Thou Art, is the state that exists. As one gradually returns to his customary and habitual state of consciousness, the jyoti is again placed in the heart and kept lighted there throughout the day.

H: In meditation on the form of God, Swami says that transition into the states of contemplation and meditation occurs naturally without the volition of the person who is meditating. But how does this tie into the meditation on light where the meditator deliberately and with volition moves the jyoti here and there?

Sai: The three stages, concentration which is below the senses, meditation which is entirely above the senses and contemplation which lies between and is partially within the senses and partially above the senses, which is on the border of each, that is the experience in genuine meditation whether the object taken be form or light. There is no essential difference. If the devotee has a form of God to which he is particularly devoted, he may merge that form into the jyoti, and that form is most attractive to him and is the object of his concentration and is seen to be within the light wherever it is seen. Or, the concentration may be just on the form of God, for God is universal in every form. Again, the object chosen is just a device to allow one to sink deeply into quietness and to allow the body, which is non-self, to fall away out of consciousness. Anything concrete, such as light, form, or sound may be chosen as the object of concentration. It is not possible to just move directly into the stage of meditation.

H: In speaking of yogas, Swami said that bhakthi yoga, devotion to God, was the only yoga worth the bother, that the others were useless. But the westerners complain that Ramakrishna Paramahamsa describes how he saw the kundalini factor

138

rise and open each chakra. What is the correct reply to this doubt?

Sai: Ramakrishna used the chakras as symbols for locations of greater sensitivity along the spinal column. There is a great deal of misunderstanding about this so-called kundalini meditation. The chakra is a wheel. There are no wheels on the spinal column. The wheel is taken as a symbol because the circulation of the blood is circular. The discs of the spinal column are also circular. By placing the 'wheel' at various points along the spinal column and giving those points particular names, one is able to fix his mind on those stipulated areas and move the mind from one to the other.

H: But Swami, how about the idea that the snake of kundalini awakens at the base of the spine and activates each chakra as it rises up?

Sai: That energy is prana. It is imagined as rising up the spine by the practice of pranayama. The practice of pranayama is dangerous unless all circumstances are exactly correct. It is not necessary, and Swami advises against it. The area between the 9th and 12th vertebrae is especially sensitive. An injury there can result in paralysis. Meditation as described by Swami is the royal road, the easy path. Why bother with other practices? For meditation to be effective there must be steady practice with no hurry and no worry. With steady practice, the person will become quiet and the state of meditation will naturally come about. To think otherwise is weakness. Success is assured. Call upon God. He will help you. He will respond and He himself will be your guru. He will guide you. He will always be at your side. Think God, see God, hear God, eat God, drink God, love God. That is the easy path, the royal road to your goal of breaking ignorance and the realization of your true nature, which is one with God.

H: Swami, the westerners are extremely interested in everything that Swami says and they think and talk about it. The fact that the breath is saying 'Sohum' 21,600 times a day has some of the people puzzled, because they say they do not experience breathing at that rate?

Sai: The 21,600 breaths per day is the typical experience. It is the average of one's life. At times of exertion or stress the breathing will be very fast; at times of peace and quiet it will be slow. Some people may have an average of more than 21,600 breaths per day. A practised yogi may average not 15 breaths per minute, but as low as 6 or 7 per minute. The slower the breathing, the longer the life span. The short-life monkey will breathe some 40 times per minute. The long-life snake will breathe 3 or 4 times per minute.

H: For us westerners, is there something of the essence, some test that could be applied to action that would point out the correct dharma for any role in life?

Sai: There is not one dharma for Indians and another for westerners. Dharma is universal. Yes. There is a test that may be applied to any action and you may thereby determine if it is according to dharma. Let not that which you do harm or injure another. This flows from the recognition that the light, which is God, is the same in every form, and if you injure another you are injuring that same light that is yourself. Dharma enables you to come to the recognition that anything that is bad for another form is also bad for you. The test for dharmic action is stated very clearly in the Christian religion. That is: Do unto others as you would have them do unto you.

H: People have their previous meditations prior to coming to a Sathya Sai Baba Center. How should they now evaluate their present meditation procedure?

Interpreter: This question is answered by Swami's description of genuine meditation. If the meditation engaged in by the new member of the Center falls short of that, then he may consider following Swami's guidance in the matter.

L

Sai: (to a group of westerners) Any doubts or questions? Spiritual questions only.

A Visitor: Why a lamp in meditation?

Sai: Why a light? If one takes from the sand it will be depleted. If each one takes from the water tank, the tank will go dry. But a thousand people can take the flame of one candle to light their candles and the flame is in no way diminished. Light a lamp or a candle. Gaze straight ahead at the flame. Then take the candle flame, the jyoti, into your heart and see it in the midst of the petals of the heart. Watch the petals of the heart unfold and see the light illumine the heart. Bad feelings cannot remain. Then move the flame to the hands and they can no longer do dark deeds. In turn move the flame in like fashion to the eyes and ears so they may henceforth take in only bright and pure sensations. Then move the light outward and into your friends, relatives and enemies, and then into animals, birds and other objects so that all are illumined by the same light. Christ said, 'All are one, be alike to everyone.' In this way you will no longer be limited to this body, but will expand throughout the universe. The world, which is now so big, will become very, very small. To expand beyond self and see that your light is the light of the universe is liberation. Liberation is not different from this.

A Visitor: To keep sitting straight is certainly not easy to do.

Sai: To sit straight is important. Between the 9th and 12th vertebrae is the life force. If the spine is injured at this point, paralysis occurs. If the body is in a straight position, as if it were wound around a straight pole, the life force may rise up through the straight body and give the quality of intense concentration to the mind. Moreover, just as a lightning rod attached to the roof of a building attracts lightning, in like fashion a perfectly straight body provides a conductor, so to speak, for divine power to enter the temple of your body and give you the strength to accomplish your task and reach your goal. As another example, the divine power is always here, just as radio signals are here. But to hear the radio music there must be an antenna. Further, if the tuning device is not properly adjusted, there will just be some sound but no music. In like fashion, the divine power, which is always present, may flow into you if the meditation is correct and the body straight.

A Visitor: How about the Brahma Mahurta meditation?

Sai: Brahma Mahurta means early morning, between three and six a.m. It means that the senses are quiet, not yet agitated by the day and the mind is quiet from sleep. But the hour should not be taken and changed around, taking one time today and another time tomorrow. A half hour in the morning and a half hour in the evening is enough for sitting meditation. If done all day long, it will lose its attraction after a couple of years. Spiritual practice should be varied for interest. Some bhajan, some repetition of the name of the Lord, some time spent in the company of spiritual people and so on. Just as in daily life some variety makes the day interesting.

H: Swami, how should the period of meditation on the jyoti be brought to a close?

Sai: First you are in the light. Then the light is in you. Finally, you are the light and the light is everywhere. Enjoy for a while, then bring the light back to the heart and hold it there for all the day. The form of God may also be included. Krishna, Rama, Jesus, Sai, as you wish. The form of God selected may be seen in the centre of the flame wherever it is carried, and then you are with God everywhere.

A Visitor: At the meeting it was mentioned, people doing other kinds of meditation should not join the Sathya Sai Baba Center.

Sai: This yoga and that yoga is not the answer. Yes, they may join even if doing other meditations. Let all unite in the one goal. God is reached only through love. Pranayama subjects the heart and the lungs to strain and pressure. The health must be good. Bhakthi yoga is best. A big mixture will only create

142

confusion. The meditation on light is safe and sure and leads directly to the goal.

A Visitor: But if one has been initiated into another meditation, Swami's book says it is a sin to change.

Sai: The goal remains the same. There is just some change in the pathway, the method employed. Meditation on light is real meditation. Light is formless, eternal, divine. It is the safe way and the sure way. But above all is love. Love is the royal highway to God. God is love. At the beginning we should carefully consider and investigate the meditation or sadhana that we propose to adopt. Who is the guru? What is the result? If then we have full confidence, full confidence that it will take us to our spiritual goal, then go ahead and stay with it. But it is a spiritual goal that we aim for, not a physical goal, not a goal at the sensory level.

A Visitor: But how can I get that self-confidence that I do not have?

Sai: To do bad things you have the self-confidence to go ahead with the bad things. The self-confidence is also there to do good things. Everyone has self-confidence.

H: That is very good.

Sai: Yes, it is important. The self-confidence is already there. If there is the interest in the good things, the self-confidence is already there to carry them out. People go to America and charge various amounts for spiritual information which belongs to everyone and for which no charge should be made. The information should not be sold and the Americans should not buy.

H: Swami, in the description of the light meditation, I was not quite sure how Swami said it had liberation as the result.

Sai: You are the light. The same light is found in others also. The body drops away and you are the light. That is liberation.

H: Does Swami mean that by means of light one expands through the entire universe and is no longer limited by body?

143

Sai: 'My' falls away. There is no longer 'My.'

H: Here is a meditation given by the Lord Himself and it takes one direct to liberation. Why would a person wish to bother with any other meditation?

Sai: Some sensory pleasure, some body result.

H: Yesterday, Swami, people got the idea that any kind of meditation could be used at a Center.

Sai: Don't worry about that. After a little while they will feel how great is the light meditation and change to this. Do not force them. Give them some time.

H: Swami says that it is a benefit of the highest order if an individual's life is such that he merits God's love. How do we directly experience that Divine Love?

Sai: In the kitchen is a sweet. Now, you must come from afar to the kitchen to enjoy the sweet. Only when you eat the food is the hunger relieved. To enjoy the sweetness of Divine Love, you must attempt to experience it directly. How to get the ability to experience the Divine Love directly? Our ancient Rishis enjoyed bliss by going to solitude and sitting with their bodies stiff and apparently lifeless. On the other hand, people are all the time shaking their heads and bodies. Such people cannot get concentration. The body is described as a temple containing the Lord. If this part of our body keeps on shaking, the contents, the mind, will also be shaking. That is why in meditation certain postures are described, and they must be maintained. When in meditation take the mind deep so as not to be distracted. The deeper the mind is taken, the less it is disturbed by the surrounding noise. In the Gita it is said that concentration precedes wisdom. If in sitting for meditation, you keep on scratching your head or your back you will not be doing the right kind of meditation. Some people sit for meditation. They simply sit, but then they wonder how soon they can move from that posture. When in meditation, concentrate on the form chosen by you, then pass into contemplation and then into meditation. Only by the three states will you get there. From concentration, one must cross the field of contemplation to enter meditation. There are the three things, the meditator, the chosen form, and the process of meditation. The three should merge and become one, and this is the state of meditation. But, if all the time you feel you are meditating, this cannot be called meditation. When there is complete attention on the form chosen, that will lead to meditation. The attention of the mind is totally removed from the body and totally concentrated on the form chosen as the object of your meditation.

H: The other day, Swami, not only were the college boys delighted at the return to Brindavan, but they were very much surprised. I was also, because Swami had said He would definitely stay at the ashram.

Sai: Baba made the decision to stay in Prasanthi Nilayam through Sivarathri. That was His sankalpa. His will is as iron. On the third day of the festival, the boys at Brindavan decorated the cows and had a procession, and their longing for Swami was so strong that Swami made a sudden decision and came to Brindavan. It might be asked, Swami's Sankalpa is as iron, how could that be changed? Well, devotion is as fire. Fire will melt iron. God is moved by devotion.

LI

H: Swami, people make conflicting statements about the use of vibhuti. Should a devotee of Swami use vibhuti as the only treatment for sickness and injury?

Sai: Do not give any importance to minor sickness and injury. In more serious matters, it is best that prayer be made to Swami. This is important. Vibhuti may or may not be used, but there should be prayer.

H: How about the help that is ordinarily available? Should a person try that first before calling to Swami?

Sai: Some people have faith in doctors, and some have faith in Swami.

H: But Swami, that is exactly the problem. People are

145

afraid that if they do anything except use vibhuti they are demonstrating lack of faith in Swami.

Sai: Actually, both can proceed together. The doctors can be consulted, and vibhuti can also be used. But, regardless of the degree of faith, it is best to pray to Swami for His Grace.

H: Some devotees go to the extreme. No matter how serious the disease or trouble, they declare they will use vibhuti only and will never go to a doctor.

Sai: If they wish to do that, they may. Swami's preference would be that ordinary means of help be given their due place.

H: Swami says that self-inquiry is 3/4ths and meditation 1/4th. What is skillful self-inquiry? Action can be either skillful or unskillful.

Sai: The devotee may not have any particular skill, but all can inquire of themselves if what they propose to do is right or wrong.

H: But are we not to take inquiry as meaning self-knowledge, knowing about what goes on within oneself?

Sai: Self-knowledge certainly is about oneself, not about the outside.

H: In finding out about oneself, Swami advises that we ask if we are the body, the mind or the intellect.

Sai: You are the witness of all these.

H: One notices other things. Every desire announces itself as "I" even though exactly contradicted by past and future desires.

Sai: Really, there are only two "I"s. One is the ego which is always identifying itself as "I," and the other "I" is the eternal witness, which is Swami. If there is awareness of the witness, the ego "I" will not bother, it does not much matter.

H: In self-inquiry, Swami, a person may notice that while his idea is that he is a free agent, yet in fact he is pushed around and made to act by all sorts of influences. Actually one is not at all free, he is like a prisoner, is he not?

Sai: That you are not free is wrong. Only up to a certain stage is one's life according to the influences that bear upon him —such as heredity, circumstances, tendencies and so on. Later on, one is superior to and free from influences.

H: But Swami, if one is a prisoner, that is the fact at the moment. If one observes this fact about himself may he then develop a very deep interest in freedom?

Sai: Very few people have these deep levels of self-inquiry. As yet they have not gone deeply into the matter. Ripeness is a factor here. In talks with devotees, these aspects of Sadhana should be brought forward and their importance indicated by your own experience.

H: One observes many emotions in himself, Swami. Some are damaging—such as anger, hatred, jealousy, depression, fear and so on. These are very strong and they come up despite one's best intentions.

Sai: This is a very important topic. It is important in America where emotions are strong and lead to violent action.

H: There seems to be a possibility, Swami, that a person can curb these dangerous emotions from going on into action.

Sai: The problem is that people have some knowledge from books, but they do not have the general knowledge of life that comes with spiritual power. With discipline, prayer to God and steady sadhana there is a spiritual power which comes up within a person, and the strength of dangerous emotions is reduced. But, even apart from that, people can and should try to restrain these harmful emotions from outward expression. There may be anger, hatred, depression raging within, but the person's outward behavior should remain peaceful. His smile should be calm. With all his strength he must resist any show of these harmful emotions. This is a topic of the highest importance. Self-inquiry, and this matter of the emotions are of the greatest importance. When talking to devotees at centers, you must deal with these two aspects of spiritual sadhana clearly and emphatically. (On previous occasions, Swami has said that dangerous and harmful impulses and emotions will vanish automatically in the Presence of God; that evil forces are products of grief, and cannot exist where there is Ananda, the happiness that arises when one loves God with all one's heart and sees Him everywhere.)

H: Another puzzling thing that may be observed is the falling away from one's goal. For example, a person may show the most steadfast determination to hold to the lotus feet of the Lord. Then a year or so later, that person has left Swami.

Sai: The reason for this is a weakness of mind in the initial stage. In the first perception of his goal, the person's mind was wavering. Had he been one-pointed and clear at first, he would not fall away from his goal. The fault lies in a wavering mind that is lacking in one-pointedness.

H: Swami, one more question, please, about household pests. The housewife is in a constant battle with ants, mosquitoes, cockroaches, etc. Unless she fights, these insects take over her home.

Sai: It is all right, they must be dealt with.

H: People are afraid they may be committing a sin against Swami if they kill these small creatures.

Sai: There is nothing wrong in keeping the home free from the assault of these small creatures. But only where you are, your area. Not outside.

H: Swami, if one ant out of a colony of ants is killed, is that killing an individual Jiva? Or, is there a sort of group Jiva whose body is the colony of ants?

Sai: There are no individual Jivas. Jiva is one only. Only one. Jiva is never injured, never killed. Bodies are many. Minds are changeable and may be affected. Bodies may be killed, may die. But Jiva is unaffected. Jiva is one and eternal.

The rule for spiritual life is to be cautious. Start carefully, drive carefully and arrive safely. (On a previous occasion, Swami said, "Be steady; be resolved. Do not commit a fault or take a false step, and then repent! Have the deliberation, the decision, the discipline first; that is better than regret for the mistake made.")

148

LII

H: May I ask a spiritual question?

Sai: Go ahead.

H: Is there something that is unique about having a physical body?

Sai: The human form is unique in that the divine force is as much as 80 per cent present. In the animal only about 15 per cent. Man can raise himself to union with God, whereas the animal can never be free of his natural state. For example, a cat can be fed some nice things, but if it sees a mouse, even while eating the food, it leaves the food and goes for the mouse. A tiger can be trained, but food made from grains does not satisfy it. The tiger's impulse to kill and eat remains.

H: But Swami, what is so unusual about it? Why should anybody wish to have a physical body?

Sai: Hislop is in Mexico or America or Puttaparthi. Without a body how would he know where he was? A stone falls. The force of gravity is unseen but is revealed by the falling stone. The body of man is necessary because it is able to reveal the unseen God. The sun, moon and stars are in space, and they move and revolve according to order and discipline. If that discipline wavered for a moment all would collapse. What maintains that discipline? It is the unseen divine force.

H: What is unique and special about having a human body?

Sai: Swami already explained that the body serves to reveal the indwelling divinity.

H: Yes, Swamiji. But I mean from the standpoint of the individual what is the value to the individual of having a body? He lives and dies, why should he care? Science says there are many planets where there will be much the same life.

Sai: In all the universe there is no other planet that has human life, or a similar life form.

H: In that case, Swami, there has to be something very special and unique about life in a physical body?

Sai: There is life throughout the universe. To God, the

universe is one. Rebirth can never be in other regions of the universe. Always the rebirth is on Earth.

H: Swami, what does that mean to the individual?

Sai: The expression of life on Earth is upward through the human to the Divine. By virtue of human birth, the next step is the full realization of the Divine. Human life is sacred and must be appreciated as having the highest value.

H: Considering the individual, Swamiji, can it be that Swami is saying that human birth is some sort of a special opportunity to get free from birth and death?

Sai: Quite right. That is the case.

H: Swamiji! Then that is it! That is the secret! That is the unique feature of being born into a body!

Sai: Yes, that is the unique feature.

H: Swami, are there other regions throughout the universe where there may also be an escape from birth and death?

Sai: Only on Earth may this take place. In no other planet or region throughout the indescribable vastness of the universe does this opportunity exist. It is unique and is limited to this earth.

H: Swami! Wonderful! Wonderful! How sacred is this Earth! How infinitely precious is human birth!

Sai: That is so. But people have no appreciation or understanding of it. They do not know.

H: Swami, may this great life secret be told to the devotees? At Sathya Sai Baba Centers, they should know that even five minutes wasted time is a tragic loss in the face of the magnificence of this human opportunity.

Sai: Yes, you may tell. The question that you have raised is of great importance, and the answer may be told.

H: Swami, the answer is divine! It is so wonderful that adequate appreciation cannot be put into words. Swamiji said that there was no rebirth from Earth to other regions of the universe. How about the reverse? Can there be a movement from the regions of the universe to Earth?

Sai: All life may aspire to human birth. But only through

the human birth may God be realized. To waste time is the greatest folly. Now and here is the individual. Now and here is the opportunity to realize the absolute goal of life. Who can be sure of the conditions and status of his next rebirth? Not even one moment of this life should be wasted.

A Visitor: Swami, I have a question. What is the best sadhana for a young person with business, family, attachments and bondage (after Swami had jokingly referred to the visitor's 8-month-old daughter as attachment-bondage-samsara)?

Sai: It is not correct to look at these things as bondage or attachment. They must be seen as "adjustment sadhana." To keep your life balanced and to give direction they are good things, and the changes you must make in your life, your daily routine—these adjustments are sadhana, not bondage.

The purpose of all sadhana is to see the good, the Divine in everything and to be able to overlook the bad, the evil. From the viewpoint of Divinity, there is no good or bad; all is Divine. But the mind sees this as good and that as bad, this as right and that as wrong. It is the mind that must be trained to see the Divine in everyone and in each difficulty.

A small example: A dead dog is on the road, crows are pecking at it. People walk by and say, "Oh, what a terrible sight and horrible smell!" But Jesus was walking by and He said, "What beautiful teeth the dog has, so white and shiny. Nobody was brushing or taking care, but still the dog kept such beautiful teeth." Jesus was showing that one can see the best qualities in even the worst situations. People who are saintly look always to the good and do not become intangled in the bad.

Another example: A knife is used by a surgeon and a knife is also used by a villain. The surgeon's cutting of a person is for his good, but the villain uses the knife for an evil purpose, a butcher may use a knife to cut meat, and a lady may use a knife to cut fruit for a salad. If all the knives are put in a circle with a magnet at the center, all the knives will be equally attracted by the magnet. The good or bad is not in the knives. God is the magnet and all men are attracted to God. Good and bad are not in a human being, but in the way the mind is used.

Do not fill the mind with thoughts of the evil actions that may be perceived in the world. The purpose of all types of sadhana is to train the mind to see the Divine in everything. That is true adjustment sadhana. This you can carry on in everything you do.

GLOSSARY

Advaita: The viewpoint that non-dualism represents the ultimate truth of God, Man and the World.

Anantapur: A town in Andhra Pradesh, South India. The location of the Sri Sathya Sai College of Arts and Science for Women.

Arjuna: The disciple of Lord Krishna to whom Krishna revealed the truth of human existence just prior to the opening battle of the Mahabharatha War. The divine discourse is known as the Bhagavad-Gita.

Ashram: Residence of a spiritual personage.

Atma: The most subtle aspect of one's being. That which is without change, unmodified, unaffected, timeless.

Atma Shakti: The force, the power of the Atma.

Avatar: The omnipresent Divine Principle, embodied yet unlimited.

Avatara: The embodied lifetime of the Avatar.

Bhagavan: Lord. God.

Bhagawan Sri Sathya Sai Baba: Acclaimed as the Avatar of the age. The omnipresent Divine Principle embodied without limitation.

Bhajans: Devotional songs.

Bhaktha: One who has love of God as the principle thrust of his life.

Bhakthi: Devotion to God. Love of God.

Bangalore: A city in South India, some fifteen miles from the Sri Sathya Sai College of Arts, Science and Commerce for Men.

Brindavan: Name given to the residence of Bhagavan Sri Sathya Sai Baba at Whitefield, some fifteen miles from Bangalore.

Dharma: Righteous action towards oneself and others, based on love for the ever-blissful and ever-loving Lord who is the Essence of all.

Dharmakshetra: Name given to the conference hall and compound in Bombay, constructed by devotees of Sri Sathya Sai.

1

Dharshan: The direct seeing of a holy person, which brings his Grace to the viewer.

Gokul: Village on the banks of the River Jumuna wherein Krishna lived his early years as one of the boys who had responsibility for the care of the village cows.

Gokulam: Name given to the farm at Puttaparthi where Sri Sathya Sai conducts a model dairy.

Gopis: The women of the village of Gokul. Supreme devotees of Krishna.

Gunas: The primary qualities of a sentient being; peaceful (Sathwa), active (Rajas) and dull (Thamas).

Guru: Spiritual preceptor.

Indra: King of the pantheon of deities.

Japamala: A string of 108 beads used in japa, the repetition of the name of God with reverence and devotion.

Jivanmukthi: The God-realized person in whom only the divine vision is active. He no longer has any identification whatsoever with his body.

Jnani: One who has direct knowledge of the highest wisdom.

Jyoti: The light and form of a flame.

Kalpataru tree: The wish-fulfilling tree, often experienced by devotees during the early years of the Sai Avatara.

Karma: Action. Also the name given to the reaction that one must experience due to his action.

Kosas: The five sheaths of embodiment.

Lakshmana: Brother of Rama.

Lanka: Island of Ceylon, Sri Lanka.

Leelas: God's sports, His play.

Mandir: Prayer Hall, Temple.

Mantrum, Mantra: A sequence of powerful words, usually Sanskrit, used to achieve a result.

Maya: An aspect of the Divine. That power of bewilderment which gives the appearance of reality to that which is unreal, and which hinders the perception of the real.

Om: The primeval sound by which God sustains the cosmos.

Paramatma: The Atma viewed in its universal aspect. God.

Prasanthi Nilayam: The abode of Bhagavan Sri Sathya Sai

Baba, north of Bangalore, beside the village of Puttaparthi.

Puttaparthi: Birthplace of Sri Sathya Sai Baba. A village in Andhra Pradesh, South India.

Rama: An Avatar of God preceeding the Avatara of Krishna. He who confers bliss. That in the heart, which is pure delight.

Ramakrishna Paramahamsa: A great saint of Bengal, 1836-1886.

Ravana: Demon king who kidnapped Sita, the consort of Rama.

Rishi: A great saint, fully knowing the omnipresence of God.

Sadhaka: One who practices the spiritual disciplines.

Sadhana: The spiritual life practiced in everyday life. Words, thoughts and actions which purify mind and heart of illusion and delusion.

Sai: The Divine Mother of all.

Sai Ram: The Divine Principle dwelling in each heart as pure delight. A name bestowed upon Bhagavan Sri Sathya Sai Baba by devotees and constantly repeated along with the visualization of the Sathya Sai form as constant sadhana.

Sankalpa: God's resolve or will.

Samadhi: A subtle state of divine bliss experienced spontaneously in spiritual practice.

Samsara: The outward tide of sensory experience. The sensory world which captures the mind and gives rise to craving and grasping and suffering. The round of birth and death which has no beginning but which has an end.

Sanyasi: A spiritual aspirant who has abandoned attachment to worldly objects and relationships and who lives apart from others. Often he is a homeless wanderer.

Saris: Traditional ladies costume worn throughout most of India.

Sastras: A category of Indian Scriptures.

Satwa, Rajas, Thamas: The three gunas or characteristics of embodied beings. Translated roughly as Peaceful, Active and Dull.

Shirdi Sai Baba: The Sai Avatara manifests as a trinity separ-

ated in relative time by the lifetimes of three embodiments;
Shirdi Sai Baba (now passed away, 1918), Sri Sathya Sai
Baba, and (still to come) Prema Sai.

Sita: The consort of Rama.

Siva: The beneficent aspect of Maheswara. The third of the
trinity of supreme deities. God.

Swami: A title of respect given to spiritual personages.

Tapas: The practice of austerities designed to weaken the
conviction that man is body.

Telugu: The native tongue of Sri Sathya Sai Baba. The language
of Andhra Pradesh.

Upanishads: A category of Indian Scriptures.

Vedanta: Vedanta proves by experience that which has been
formulated, specifically, Advaita (non-dualism).

Vedas: The breath of God, from which knowledge is gained of
the unseen support of the seen.

Vedic: That which derives from the Vedas. (An adjective).

Vivekananda: Favorite disciple of Ramakrishna Paramahamsa.

Yogi: A spiritual aspirant who seeks union with God by means
of one or more specific mental and physical disciplines
which are traditional and which are known by the title of
yoga.

Yugas: The four phases through which life moves to complete
a world cycle.

Centers for the study and practice of the teachings of Sathya Sai Baba have been established worldwide. About one hundred Centers are located in the United States. Many are listed in local telephone directories under the title: "Sathya Sai Baba Center. . . ."

For further information about the location of a Center in your area, or for a list of publications about the life and teachings of Sathya Sai Baba, you can write the Sathya Sai Baba Information Center, P.O. Box 7722, San Diego, California 92107